MEDICAL TECHNICIANS

PRACTICAL CAREER GUIDES

Series Editor: Kezia Endsley

MEDICAL TECHNICIANS

A Practical Career Guide

KEZIA ENDSLEY

ROWMAN & LITTLEFIELD
Lanham • Boulder • New York • London

Published by Rowman & Littlefield
An imprint of The Rowman & Littlefield Publishing Group, Inc.
4501 Forbes Boulevard, Suite 200, Lanham, Maryland 20706
www.rowman.com

86-90 Paul Street, London EC2A 4NE, United Kingdom

British Library Cataloguing in Publication Information Available

Library of Congress Cataloging-in-Publication Data

Names: Endsley, Kezia, 1968– author.
Title: Medical technicians : a practical career guide / Kezia Endsley.
Description: Lanham, MD : Rowman & Littlefield, 2022. | Series: Practical career guides | Includes bibliographical references. | Summary: *"Medical Technicians: A Practical Career Guide* covers the steps you need to take to have a career in this field and includes interviews with professionals currently working in this field"—Provided by publisher.
Identifiers: LCCN 2021043653 (print) | LCCN 2021043654 (ebook) | ISBN 9781538159286 (paperback) | ISBN 9781538159293 (epub)
Subjects: LCSH: Medical technology—Vocational guidance. | Biomedical technicians—Vocational guidance.
Classification: LCC R855.3 .E67 2022 (print) | LCC R855.3 (ebook) | DDC 610.69—dc23
LC record available at https://lccn.loc.gov/2021043653
LC ebook record available at https://lccn.loc.gov/2021043654

Contents

Introduction

Welcome to a Career as a Medical Technician/Technologist!

*I*f you are interested in a career in health care and are curious to learn what medical technicians/technologists do, you've come to the right book. The "med tech" field is a varied, flexible, exciting, rewarding, and highly in-demand career. Some med techs work with physicians, lab managers, and other technologists to perform tests on a variety of specimens, including blood and other bodily tissues. Some others operate technical, complicated machines to create images that help doctors diagnose medical conditions. For example, a CT technologist operates a computerized tomography (CT) machine. The CT takes images of the body along several axes to help diagnose bone and joint issues, or find tumors and cancer. In this book, you'll learn about all these different career options for someone interested in the med tech umbrella.

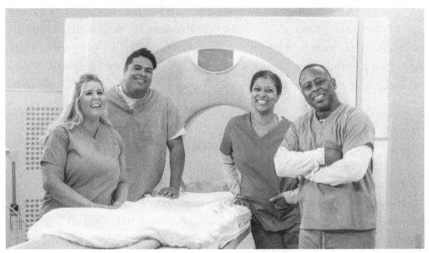

A career as a medical technologist is a career in health care: you will succeed and enjoy it more if you have a desire to help people.
kali9/E +/Getty Images

There is a lot of good news about this field, and it's a very smart career choice for anyone with a passion to help people. It's a great career for people who get energy from working with other people and want to help others get and stay healthy. Job demand is high, and there continues to be a shortage of medical technologists entering the workforce compared to the rising need.

When considering any career, your goal should be to find your specific nexus of interest, passion, and job demand. Yes, it is important to consider job outlook and demand, educational requirements, and other such practical matters, but remember that you'll be spending a large portion of your life at whatever career you choose, so you should also find something that you enjoy doing and are passionate about. Of course, it can make the road easier to walk if you choose something that's in demand and lucrative. That's where the medical technician profession really shines!

The Difference Between Medical Technicians and Medical Technologists

Medical *technicians* and *technologists* are related occupations with a lot of overlap, but the education requirements and the job duties are often very different. To become a *technologist*, you usually need a bachelor's degree and a more extensive knowledgebase than a technician. A *technician* typically needs an associate degree in medical lab technology or a related field and serves in more entry-level positions. In this book, we mostly use the terms interchangeably and focus instead on the areas of medicine they serve.

Careers in Medical Technology

There are so many different roles that we can't possibly cover them all here—check out the sidebar on the following page to see just some of the many options. In this book, you'll meet several medical technologists and talk about careers in med tech from many different points of view.

This book covers the following main areas of interest and focus, based on their roles and responsibilities:

A CAREER BY ANY OTHER NAME?

Anesthesia technician
Cardiovascular technician
CT technician
Cytogenetic technician
Dental technician
Dialysis technician
EEG technician
EKG technician
Emergency medical technician (EMT)
Laboratory technician
Medical Equipment technician
MRI technician
Nuclear medicine technologist
Pharmacy technician
Phlebotomist
Radiation therapist
Radiologic technologist
Radiology technician
Sonographer
Surgical technician
Ultrasound technician
Ultrasound technician
Veterinary technician
X-Ray technologist

- Cardiovascular technologists (ECG or EKG technicians)
- Nuclear medicine technologists
- Phlebotomy technicians
- Laboratory technicians
- Surgical technologists
- Radiologic technologists (X-ray, MRI, and CT technicians)

In addition to these are the dental technician and the veterinary technician. If you're interested specifically in either of those fields, there are books in the series devoted specifically to them (*Dental Assistants and Hygienists: A Practical Career Guide* and *Veterinary Technicians and Assistants: A Practical Career Guide*). Likewise, EMTs (emergency medical technicians) are covered in the book *First Responders: A Practical Career Guide.* Don't forget to check out those options too!

So, what exactly do these technicians do on the job, day in and day out? What kind of skills and educational background do you need to succeed? How much can you expect to make, and what are the pros and cons of being a medical technician? How do you avoid burnout and deal with stress? Is this even the right career path for you? This book can help you answer these questions and more!

> "I take care of people. That's the number one thing I do. People come to me feeling vulnerable. I enjoy playing a part of their health care in terms of diagnosing issues and helping them. Interacting with the patients and meeting new people every day is the best part of my job!" —Stacia Mellinger, X-ray technologist

For each of these roles, the book covers the pros and cons, the educational requirements, projected annual wages, personality traits that match, working conditions and expectations, and more. You'll even read interviews from real professionals working as medical technicians. The goal is for you to learn enough about the field in all its variations to give you a clear view as to which aspect, if any, is a good fit for you. And, if you still have questions, we will also point you to resources where you can learn even more.

Here is an important note to consider: regardless of the career you choose, if it's within the health care umbrella, you need to have a lifelong curiosity and love of learning. Your education won't be over once you finish your degree or certification. In fact, maintaining current certifications and meeting or exceeding continuing education requirements (usually set forth by some governing board and/or by state regulations where you practice) are all very important in all the health care fields, including in medical technology.

The Market Today

The good news is that the US Bureau of Labor Statistics forecasts that all these fields enjoy a growth much faster than the average profession (see https://www .bls.gov/emp/ for a full list of employment projections). Let's look at each job area in detail:

- *Cardiovascular technologists (ECG or EKG technicians):* Expected to grow 12 percent from 2019 to 2029, which is much faster than the average for all occupations[1]
- *Nuclear medicine technologists:* Expected to grow 5 percent from 2019 to 2029, faster than the average for all occupations[2]
- *Phlebotomy technicians:* Expected to grow 17 percent from 2019 to 2029, faster than the average for all occupations[3]
- *Laboratory technicians:* Expected to grow 7 percent from 2019 to 2029, faster than the average for all occupations[4]
- *Surgical technologists:* Expected to grow 7 percent from 2019 to 2029, faster than the average for all occupations[5]
- *Radiologic technologists (X-ray, MRI, and CT technicians):* Expected to grow 7 percent from 2019 to 2029, faster than the average for all occupations[6]

The demand for these jobs continues to grow in the United States due to many factors:

- The United States has a large elderly population. As the generation of "baby boomers" continues to age, the need to diagnose medical conditions—such as blood clots, cancer, and heart disease—increases.[7]
- Growing diseases, disorders, and illnesses, including Alzheimer's disease, cerebral palsy, attention-deficit/hyperactivity disorder (ADHD), and autism spectrum disorders, all demand continuing services from health care providers, including medical technicians.
- Hospitals and health care professionals are emphasizing preventive care (often including imaging and other tests) to help patients recover from cardiovascular and pulmonary diseases and to improve their overall health.

- Treatments in injury prevention and detection continue to evolve and be more complicated. These include MRIs, PET and CAT/CT scans, X-rays, and more.

Chapter 1 covers lots more about the job prospects and breaks down the numbers for each area into more detail.

What Does This Book Cover?

The goal of this book is to cover all aspects of your search and explain how this profession works and how you can excel in it. Here's a breakdown of the chapters:

- Chapter 1 explains the four different types of med tech roles in the United States at this time that are covered in this book. You'll learn about what people do in these roles in their day-to-day work, the environments where you can find these people working, some pros and cons about this career path, the average salaries of these jobs, and the outlook in the future for these roles.
- Chapter 2 explains in detail the educational requirements of these different jobs, from four-year bachelor's to two-year associate degrees, as well as the various certifications you'll need. You will learn how to go about getting experience (in the form of shadowing, internships, and fieldwork) in these fields before you enter college as well as during your college years.
- Chapter 3 explains all the aspects of college and postsecondary schooling that you'll want to consider as you move forward. You will learn how to get the best education for the best deal. You will also learn a little about scholarships and financial aid and how the SAT and ACT tests work.
- Chapter 4 covers all aspects of the interviewing and résumé-writing processes, including writing a stellar résumé and cover letter, interviewing to your best potential, dressing for the part, how to communicate effectively and efficiently, and more.

Where Do You Start?

The field of medical technology is so vast and varied that you can approach your career from many angles. Are you more interested in working in a lab with blood and tissues, or would you rather operate an MRI machine and help people that way? Do you want to work in a high-stress, high-stakes, exciting environment like emergency medicine, or are you more suited for steady work where you build rapport with the same patients over years, such as in an office setting? Do you want to specialize in one area of care, such as X-ray, or would you prefer to work as a generalist? The options are nearly endless, and you can change your focus as you age and advance in your health care career.

The good news is that you don't need to know the answers to these questions yet. In order to find the best fit as a med tech, you need to understand how they work. That's where you'll start in chapter 1.

Starting your career journey can be daunting, but this book can help!
sergeichekman/iStock/Getty Images

Why Choose a Career as a Medical Technician/Technologist?

You learned in the introduction that the field of medical technology is a large, healthy, and growing career field. You also learned a little bit about how it's split into different roles, depending on your degree, level of schooling, and interest. You also were reminded that it's important to pursue a career that you enjoy, are good at, and are passionate about. You will spend a lot of your life working; it makes sense to find something you enjoy doing. Of course, you want to make money and support yourself while doing it. If you love the idea of helping people for a living, you've come to the right book.

As the introduction explained, *medical technologists* and *medical technicians* have related job duties, such as performing tests for health care professionals, but the level of complexity differs between the jobs. They are both responsible for analyzing body fluids to check for irregularities, for example. Technicians, with less experience and a less advanced degree, might do the data entry and interact with patients by collecting blood samples. A technologist, who might have a bachelor's degree or many years on the job, also does these things, but their job goes a step further. They also analyze samples and might weigh in on the meaning of the results. Medical technologists perform more complicated, manual tests, whereas technicians conduct simpler tests using automated processes.

As a reminder, this book covers these main fields of medical technology:

- Cardiovascular technologists (ECG or EKG technicians)
- Nuclear medicine technologists
- Phlebotomy technicians
- Laboratory technicians
- Surgical technologists
- Radiologic technologists (X-ray, MRI, and CT technicians)

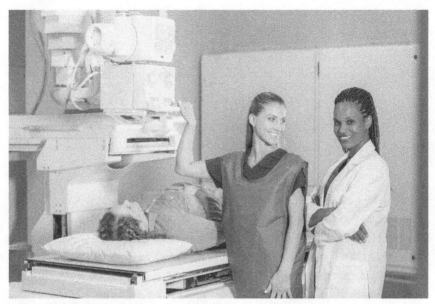

Medical technicians assist doctors with medical diagnoses by performing tests on patients.
kali9/iStock/Getty Images

In this chapter, we break out these areas and cover the basics of each. After reading this chapter, you should have a good understanding of each role and can begin to determine if one of them is a good fit for you. Let's start with cardiovascular technologists.

Cardiovascular Technologists

Cardiovascular technologists assist doctors in diagnosing *cardiac* (heart) and *peripheral vascular* (blood vessel) disease or problems through the imaging programs they run on patients. They work in a cardiac "cath" lab and perform various procedures, including stent implants (a metal or plastic tube inserted to keep the passageway open), cardiac pacemakers and defibrillators, and other tests to diagnose heart disease.[1] Such labs can be in hospitals, doctors' offices, and medical and diagnostic laboratories. Cardiovascular technologists who work in hospital settings also take emergency calls and participate in saving the lives of people who are having a heart attack.

Cardiovascular technologists who specialize in electrocardiograms (ECGs or EKGs), stress testing, and Holter monitors (another kind of EKG) are known as cardiographic or ECG technicians.[2]

Note: An *electrocardiogram* (ECG or EKG) is a simple test that check a patient's heart rhythm and electrical activity. Sensors attached to the skin detect the electrical signals produced by the heart each time it beats. Check out the glossary for other medical terms mentioned in this book!

Cardiovascular *technologists* usually need an associate degree or bachelor's degree in sonography or in cardiovascular and vascular technology. To become a cardiovascular *technician*, you typically need a high school diploma and can be trained on the job. You may also choose to attend a certificate program or earn an associate degree. One-year certificate programs are available from colleges and some hospitals.[3]

Tip: Employers typically prefer graduates of programs accredited by the Commission on Accreditation of Allied Health Education Programs (CAAHEP)—see *www.caahep.org*.

Chapters 2 and 3 cover these educational and professional certification requirements in more detail.

MAIN RESPONSIBILITIES

Cardiovascular technologists:

- Explain the testing procedures to patients to reduce their anxiety
- Run EKGs and other tests (such as phonocardiograms and echocardiograms) to check the health of a patient's heart
- Run stress tests on patients to check heart function
- Assist doctors with stent implants, cardiac pacemakers, and defibrillators
- Ready patients and assist doctors during procedures such as cardiac catheterization and open-heart surgery

- Operate carotid ultrasounds to look for blocked arteries farther away from the heart
- Write up reports of diagnostic procedures for the doctors
- Watch gauges, recorders, and video screens of the system during the imaging process[4]

HOW HEALTHY IS THE CARDIOVASCULAR TECHNOLOGIST JOB MARKET?

The Bureau of Labor Statistics is part of the US Department of Labor (see https://www.bls.gov). It tracks statistical information about thousands of careers in the United States. For anyone studying to become a cardiovascular technologist, the news is great! Employment is expected to grow 12 percent in the decade 2019 to 2029, which is much faster than the average profession.[5] Like most health care fields, cardiovascular technologists are expected to be in increasing demand as the generation of "baby boomers" continues to age and our population continues to struggle with health issues.

These statistics show just how promising this career is now and in the foreseeable future:

- *Education:* A bachelor's degree is preferred, although an associate degree is also acceptable in many places, especially at the entry level. Most employers prefer to hire diagnostic imaging workers with professional certification as well.
- *2020 median pay:* $70,380.
- *Job outlook 2019–2029:* 12 percent (much faster than average).
- *Work environment:* Largely in hospitals, physicians' offices, or medical and diagnostic laboratories.[6]

Nuclear Medicine Technologists

Nuclear medicine technologists prepare radioactive drugs and administer them to patients for imaging or treatment. They support physicians, who diagnose, care for, and treat patients. They also may act as emergency responders in the event of a nuclear disaster.

To become a nuclear medicine technologist, you typically need an associate degree from an accredited nuclear medicine technology program. Formal education programs in nuclear medicine technology or a related health care field lead to a certificate, an associate degree, or a bachelor's degree. Your job prospects will be better if you become certified, and you might also need to be licensed, depending on where you practice.

MAIN RESPONSIBILITIES

Nuclear medicine technologists do the following:

- Explain medical procedures to the patients and answer any questions
- Follow safety procedures to protect themselves and the patients from unnecessary radiation exposure
- Prepare radioactive drugs and administer them to patients
- Maintain and operate imaging equipment
- Keep detailed records of procedures
- Follow proper procedures for radiation disposal[7]

Nuclear medicine technologists work with radioactive drugs, known as *radiopharmaceuticals*, to help physicians diagnose issues.[8] For example, they might inject radiopharmaceuticals into the bloodstream of a patient with foot pain and then use special scanning equipment that captures images of the bones. A radiologist would then interpret the scan results, based on the concentration of radioactivity appearing in the image, to identify the source of the patient's pain.

Nuclear medicine technologists also inject radiopharmaceuticals in exact doses to specific areas, such as into tumors, to treat medical conditions. Internal radiation treatment may be used in conjunction with, or as an alternative to, surgery.

HOW HEALTHY IS THE JOB MARKET FOR NUCLEAR MEDICINE TECHNOLOGISTS?

The Bureau of Labor Statistics reports that employment for nuclear medicine technologists is expected to grow 5 percent in the decade 2019 to 2029, which is faster than the average.

These statistics show just how promising this career is now and in the fore-seeable future:[9]

- *Education*: Associate degree in nuclear medicine technology or related health field.
- *2020 median pay:* $79,590.
- *Job outlook 2019–2029:* 5 percent (faster than average).
- *Work environment:* Most nuclear medicine technologists work in hospitals. Others work in doctors' offices, laboratories, or imaging clinics.

Phlebotomy Technicians

The primary responsibilities of a phlebotomy technician (or *phlebotomist*) center around blood: they draw blood from patients for tests, transfusions, research, and blood donations. They interact with patients and help calm them during what can be a nerve-racking procedure for many. They may explain their work to patients and provide help if patients have adverse reactions after their

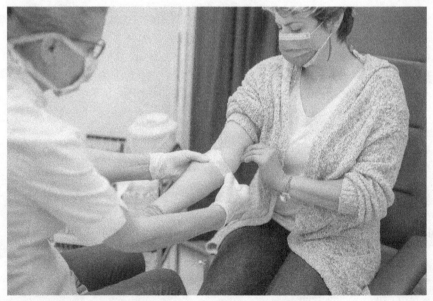

Phlebotomists should have a good manner with patients, in order to calm them during blood draws if necessary.
zoranm/E +/Getty Images

blood is drawn. In order to avoid causing infection and spreading disease, they must keep their work area and instruments sanitary.

Phlebotomists typically have a certification from a phlebotomy program.[10] These certification programs include classroom sessions and laboratory work, and they cover lessons in anatomy, physiology, and medical terminology. These types of programs are available from community colleges, vocational schools, and technical schools and usually take less than one year to complete. It is also possible in some areas to enter the occupation with a high school diploma and be trained to be a phlebotomist on the job.

MAIN RESPONSIBILITIES

Phlebotomists typically do the following:[11]

- Draw blood from patients and donors
- Reassure patients and donors to help them feel less nervous
- Verify a patient's or donor's identity and match that with the correct blood draw
- Properly label the drawn blood
- Enter patient and medical information into a database
- Clean and maintain medical instruments such as needles, test tubes, and blood vials
- Keep work areas sanitary

HOW HEALTHY IS THE JOB MARKET FOR PHLEBOTOMISTS?

The Bureau of Labor Statistics reports that employment for phlebotomists is expected to grow 17 percent in the decade 2019 to 2029, which is much faster than the average. Diagnostic tests are on the rise, and hospitals and doctors' offices need phlebotomists to draw the blood for those tests.

These statistics show how this career fares, now and in the foreseeable future:[12]

- *Education:* Postsecondary nondegree certificate.
- *2020 median pay:* $36,320.
- *Job outlook 2019–2029:* 17 percent (much faster than average).
- *Work environment:* Phlebotomists work in hospitals, medical and diagnostic laboratories, blood donor centers, and doctors' offices.

Laboratory Technicians

Clinical laboratory technologists (also known as *medical laboratory scientists*) and clinical laboratory technicians perform tests on biological samples they get from patients. They may collect those samples, or they may receive them from another collection site. They analyze body fluids such as blood and urine, tissues, and other substances and record their findings. Depending on the type of lab they work in, they might prepare slides of body cells and examine them under a microscope for irregularities related to cancer, examine and identify bacteria and other microorganisms in a patient's blood, or classify blood and prepare it and its components for transfusions.[13]

Clinical laboratory technologists typically need a bachelor's degree in medical technology or a related life sciences field, such as biology. Technicians usually need an associate degree or a postsecondary certificate. Many states require technologists and technicians to be licensed; these requirements vary by state and specialty. Visit the American Society for Clinical Laboratory Science site at http://www.ascls.org/ to find out more about what's required where you live.[14]

MAIN RESPONSIBILITIES

Lab techs do the following:

- Evaluate body fluids, such as blood, urine, and tissue samples, and record their findings
- Investigate blood samples for use in transfusions by identifying the number of cells, the cell morphology or the blood group, blood type, and compatibility with other blood types
- Work with sophisticated laboratory equipment, such as microscopes and cell counters
- Operate automated equipment and computerized instruments
- Collect data from medical tests and enter results into a patient's medical record
- Discuss their results and findings with doctors[15]

Technicians and technologists both perform tests and procedures. However, technologists perform more complicated tests and laboratory procedures than technicians do. For example, technologists may prepare specimens and perform detailed manual tests, whereas technicians run more routine, automated tests. Laboratory technicians usually work under the supervision of laboratory technologists.

HOW HEALTHY IS THE JOB MARKET FOR LABORATORY TECHS?

The Bureau of Labor Statistics reports that employment for lab tech roles is expected to grow 7 percent in the decade 2019 to 2029, which is faster than the average. Your job prospects will be best if you complete an accredited education program and earn a professional certification.

These statistics show just how promising this career path is now and in the foreseeable future:[16]

- *Education*: Bachelor's degree.
- *2020 median pay:* $54,180.
- *Job outlook 2019–2029:* 7 percent (faster than average).
- *Work environment:* The majority of lab techs work in hospital settings. Others work in medical and diagnostic laboratories or doctors' offices.

Surgical Technologists

Surgical technologists, often also called *operating room technicians*, assist surgeons during operations. They prepare operating rooms by setting up surgical instruments and equipment and preparing sterile solutions and medications. They help doctors during surgeries by passing the sterile instruments and supplies to them. They might also hold retractors, hold internal organs in place during a procedure, or set up robotic surgical equipment.[17]

After the operation is complete, surgical technologists may apply bandages and other dressings to the incision site. They may also transfer patients to recovery rooms and restock operating rooms after a procedure.

You'll typically need a diploma, certificate, or associate degree from an accredited surgical technology program. Many community colleges and vocational schools, as well as some universities and hospitals, offer accredited programs. These programs can range in length from several months to two years.

There are about 500 surgical technologist programs accredited by the Commission on Accreditation of Allied Health Education Programs (http://www.caahep.org/).[18]

MAIN RESPONSIBILITIES

Surgical technologists do the following:

- Get operating rooms ready for surgery
- Sterilize equipment and make sure that there are proper supplies for the surgery
- Prepare patients for surgery, such as by disinfecting incision sites
- Help surgeons during surgery by passing them instruments and other sterile supplies
- Count supplies, such as surgical instruments, to ensure that no foreign objects are left in patients
- Help maintain a sterile environment to prevent patient infection[19]

HOW HEALTHY IS THE JOB MARKET FOR SURGICAL TECHNOLOGISTS?

These statistics show just how promising this career path is now and in the foreseeable future:[20]

- *Education*: Certification or associate degree.
- *2020 median pay:* $49,710.
- *Job outlook 2019–2029:* 7 percent (faster than average).
- *Work environment:* Most surgical techs work in hospitals and outpatient care centers.

Radiologic Technologists

Radiologic technologists use different types of medical diagnostic equipment to run scans on patients for diagnostic purposes. They may choose to specialize in one area of imaging, such as in X-ray, mammography, MRI (magnetic resonance imaging), or CT (computed tomography) imaging. For example, MRI technologists use magnetic resonance imaging scanners. They inject patients

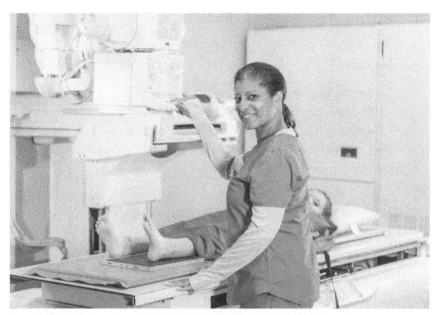

Being an X-ray tech requires excellent technical skills and good people skills.
kali9/E +/Getty Images

with dyes so that the images will show up on the scanner. The scanners use magnetic fields in combination with the dye to produce images that a doctor can use to diagnose medical problems.[21]

MAIN RESPONSIBILITIES

Radiologic technologists do the following:

- Run and maintain the imaging equipment, such as magnetic resonance imaging scanners or computed tomography scanners
- Prepare patients for procedures, including taking a medical history and covering areas that do not need to be imaged
- Position patients and equipment in order to get the correct images
- Direct the computerized equipment to take the images
- Work with doctors to evaluate the images and to determine whether more images need to be taken
- Keep detailed patient records[22]

HOW HEALTHY IS THE JOB MARKET FOR RADIOLOGIC TECHNOLOGISTS?

These statistics show just how promising this career path is now and in the foreseeable future:[23]

- *Education:* Associate degree.
- *2020 median pay:* $63,710.
- *Job outlook 2019–2029:* 7 percent (faster than average).
- *Work environment:* Work in hospitals, outpatient care centers, and medical and diagnostic labs.

THE PROS AND CONS OF BEING A MEDICAL TECHNOLOGIST

The jury is in: medical technologists and technicians enjoy a promising and lucrative career! This field is healthy and stable, as you've learned specifically in this chapter. Employment opportunities are increasing in this area. If you choose to become a medical technologist, you'll enjoy a good salary and job security. In addition to security, the profession typically affords flexible work hours, especially after you have a few years under your belt. Because medical technicians are needed all over the country (and beyond), you will find it much easier to secure a new job after a move as well.

Also, because it's practiced in many different settings and because the purpose of imaging can vary greatly, your day-to-day job duties frequently change, which means it's harder to get bored or feel stuck doing the same job all the time. The routines are never boring. Even though you may be using the same machine most of the time, you'll be exposed to different injuries and diseases, as well as other issues that require a scan. Each day can bring a new challenge and a new mystery to solve.

Maybe the greatest "pro" associated with this career is that you'll also be able to help people during their time of need. It's a career you can feel good about because you are helping people.

Despite its many advantages, there are a few "cons" to consider as well. One issue to keep in mind is the *physicality* of the job. You will be on your feet and working hands-on with patients all day. This can lead to chronic physical issues, such as back pain, that you need to be ready to manage and treat.

> "You need empathy and compassion, flexibility, creativity, and must be able to think out of the box. Not everything is a standard out-of-the-book case. You have to be flexible about what you might find, what patients need from you, emergencies that change your personal plans, etc." —Stacey Bettegnies, assistant professor in radiography

If you're working in a hospital or any emergency care environment, you'll likely be called to the ER to run scans on people who need immediate, life-saving care. They may have been in bad accidents, were injured during a fight, were abused or beaten, and more. You may even be physically attacked by the very patients you're trying to help. These can be emotionally traumatic situations to have to deal with, and you have to keep your cool and be professional throughout the process.

In addition to physical stress, the mental stress of caring for sick people is also well documented. Even though working with others can be a great source of joy and satisfaction, dealing with patients can also be a source of stress—whether it's patients with terminal illness, patients who don't comply with their treatment regimen, or overall difficult or noncomplying patients, the burden of caring for human beings can take its toll.

And, as with all health care professions, there is always a risk of infection and exposure to viruses and germs when working around patient populations, especially if you work in a hospital or health care facility. There's also the potential for needle sticks during procedures and IV insertions. For these reasons, following proper protocols and practicing self-care are very important.

Am I Right for This Profession?

Ask yourself these questions:

- Do I like meeting, talking with, and helping people?
- Do I feel empathy and concern for others in need?

- Do I feel comfortable dealing with bodily fluids, such as blood and urine?
- Am I comfortable around people who are sick or disabled?
- Am I detail oriented and able to handle multiple tasks as once?
- Am I a critical thinker and can act quickly on my feet?
- Am I ready to spend most of my working day on my feet?
- Do I enjoy learning about the biology of the human body?
- Do I mind touching people I don't know or could I learn to be comfortable with this idea?
- Can I handle the emotional issues that accompany dealing with people with medical emergencies or chronic physical or cognitive issues?

If the answer to any of these questions is an adamant no, you might want to consider a different path. However, keep in mind that many of these skills can be learned and honed if you have the right attitude and a passion for health care.

Being a med tech involves collaborative and cooperative work with the whole medical team.
monkeybusinessimage/iStock/Getty Images

===

HEIDI BRYANT: CT TECHNICIAN

Heidi Bryant graduated from a hospital-based program in radiology in 1997. She began her career working as an X-ray technician. In 2000, a job opened in the CT department. At that time, there wasn't specific modality training like there is now, so she was trained on the job. She has worked for the same organization her entire career, at Community Howard Regional Health in Kokomo, Indiana. She has been the lead CT tech for the last two years.

Can you explain how you became interested in a career as a CT technician?

I knew I was interested in working in health care or in the medical field in some capacity, but I knew that I didn't want to be a doctor or a nurse. I shadowed with someone who was an X-ray tech. I was really fascinated by the imaging and the visual aspect of the disease process.

Can you talk about your current position? What does a CT scan technician do?

I have been the lead CT tech for the last two years at Howard Community Hospital. We have an outpatient patient every half hour. In between that, we also do inpatient CTs and emergency CTs, as well as add-ins. I work three 12-hour shifts each week. CT itself is very fast-paced. The exams can range between 5 and 20 minutes long. I see about 75 people a day.

I also need to do contrast for some of our studies. I start the IVs with the contrast dyes in them, which highlight the blood vessels. Occasionally, I do lung and liver biopsies, which are much more time-consuming. These take one to one and a half hours. I also run the CAT scan and do imaging while the doctor places a drain properly, such as to relieve post-op infections.

As CT technicians, we can look at blood flow, organs, bones, and soft tissue. We do head CTs for strokes. CT is similar to MRI (in that it does cross-sectional images), and it can rule out bleeding, infection, fractures, and more. It's beneficial to doctors to help diagnose what's really going on without having to operate.

CT changes quickly. If you are in a hospital room setting, emergency room patients can be in critical condition and it's fast paced. My day-to-day is varied and different depending on what's going on in the hospital. If you work in an imaging center, those jobs are more routine. I personally find the hospital setting a little more interesting and exciting because you deal with trauma, and it's different every day. I like the wide variety.

Do you think your education prepared you for your job?

At the time, I went through a hospital-based program with clinical training, which was very hands-on, and I saw a lot. The classwork was good too, but the clinical time is very good. The hospital had its own radiology program and you worked directly there during your clinicals.

What's the best part of your job?

I still enjoy helping patients and explaining the procedures to them so they aren't scared and intimidated. I enjoy doing what I can to bring patients comfort while they are with me.

What about your profession do you find especially challenging?

After you have done it for a while, you can start to see abnormalities and you can see that things are getting worse, such as with cancer patients. You may scan them every three months or so. You get to know them and get attached to them, yet you can see that the cancer is coming back. But you still have to be positive and encouraging, and that can be hard.

What are some characteristics of a good medical technician?

You have to be detail oriented, be empathetic, and ask lots of questions. You also have to be patient and tolerant of people.

What advice do you have for young people considering this career?

Try to job shadow if at all possible. If you enter an X-ray program, you can then do specialized areas from there. When you are in regular X-ray school, you get to spend a week or so in each area and they are all different. So, try them all and consider which you like best. That was really helpful to me.

How can a young person prepare for this career while in high school?

Take anatomy and physiology classes for sure, and in general, be interested in your science and math classes. If you can volunteer at a hospital, find out if you like helping people who are sick or in need. There is something for everyone, and they are all different. You can even go into teaching X-ray programs. It's an extremely interesting career—the people, the patients, and the scans.

I am really happy I did it. It's also flexible. I work three 12-hour shifts each week. And every third week, I have six days off. I like the three-twelves—it was nice when my kids were little too. That's the hospital setting, of course. Working at an imaging center or an outpatient clinic or med check will be different. We even have people who only work weekend options, and they get paid better.

Characteristics of a Great Med Tech

Regardless of the source you turn to, you'll find the same basic characteristics used to describe a great med tech. They all boil down to these:

- Be detail oriented and organized
- Be empathetic
- Have good interpersonal skills
- Be adaptable
- Be emotionally stable
- Have physical and mental endurance
- Be hard working
- Enjoy cooperative and collaborative work
- Feel comfortable working with the human body
- Get energy from being around others

If you pursue a career that fundamentally conflicts with the person you are, you won't be good at it, and you won't be happy. Don't make that mistake. Need help in determining your key personality factors? Take a career counseling questionnaire to find out more. You can find many online or ask your school guidance counselor for reputable sources.

Summary

In this chapter, you learned a lot about the different roles that medical technologists can take in the health care world—as cardiovascular technologists, nuclear medicine technologists, phlebotomy technicians, laboratory technicians, surgical technologists, and radiologic technologists.

You've learned about what they do in their day-to-day work, the environments where you can find these people working, some pros and cons about each career path, the average salaries of these jobs, and the outlook in the future for all these careers. You hopefully even contemplated some questions about whether your personal likes and preferences meld well with these roles. At this time, you should have a good idea what each role looks like. Are you starting to get excited about one area of med tech over another? If not, that's okay, as there's still time.

An important take-away from this chapter is that no matter which of these areas you might pursue, keep in mind that getting certified and meeting the continuing education requirements can give you a leg up (and are many times required). Advances in understanding in the fields of medicine, oncology, nutrition, traumatic injury, and more are continuous, and it's vitally important that you keep apprised of what's happening in your field. You need to have a lifelong love of learning to succeed in health care.

In chapter 2, we dive into forming a plan for your future. We cover everything there is to know about educational requirements, certifications, internship and clinical requirements, and more about each of these roles. You'll learn about finding summer jobs and making the most of volunteer work as well. The goal is for you to set yourself apart—and above—the rest.

2

Forming a Career Plan

*N*ow that you have some idea about what a med tech does and the type of environment they work in, or maybe you even know that you want to start pursuing this career, it's time to formulate a career plan. For you organized folks out there, this can be a helpful and energizing process. If you're not a naturally organized person, or perhaps the idea of looking ahead and building a plan to adulthood scares you, you are not alone. That's what this chapter is for.

After we talk about ways to develop a career plan (there is more than one way to do this!), the chapter dives into the various educational requirements of this profession. Finally, we will look at how you can gain experience through internships, volunteering, clinic work, shadowing, and more. Yes, experience will look good on your résumé, and in some cases, it's even required, but even more important, getting out there and experiencing a job in various settings is the best way to determine if it's really something that you will enjoy or not. When you find a career that you truly enjoy, it will rarely feel like work at all.

If you still aren't sure if this career is right for you, try a self-assessment questionnaire or a career aptitude test. There are many good ones on the web. As an example, the career-resource website, monster.com, includes its favorite free self-assessment tools at https://www.monster.com/career-advice/article/best-free-career-assessment-tools. The Princeton Review also has a very good aptitude test geared toward high schoolers at https://www.princetonreview.com/quiz/career-quiz.

Your ultimate goal should be to match your personal interests/goals with your preparation plan for college/careers. Practice articulating your plans and goals to others. Once you feel comfortable doing this, you likely have a good grasp of your goals and the plan to reach them.

YOUR PASSIONS, ABILITIES, AND INTERESTS: IN JOB FORM!

Think about how you've done at school and how things have worked out at any temporary or part-time jobs you've had so far. What are you really good at, in your opinion? And what have other people told you you're good at? What are you not very good at right now, but you would like to become better at? What are you not very good at, and you're okay with not getting better at?

Now forget about work for a minute. In fact, forget about needing to ever have a job again. You won the lottery—congratulations. Now answer these questions: What are your favorite three ways of spending your time? For each one of those things, can you describe why you think you in particular are attracted to it? If you could get up tomorrow and do anything you wanted all day long, what would it be? These questions can be fun, but can also lead you to your true passions. The next step is to find the job that sparks your passions.

Planning the Plan

You are on a fact-finding mission of sorts. A career fact-finding plan, no matter what the field, should include these main steps:

- Take some time to consider and jot down your interests and personality traits. Are you a people person or do you get energy from being alone? Are you creative or analytical? Are you outgoing or shy? Are you organized or creative, or a little of both? Take a career-counseling questionnaire (found online or in your guidance counselor's office) to find out more. Consider whether your personal likes and preferences meld well with the jobs you are considering.
- Find out as much as you can about the day-to-day of the job. In what kinds of environments is it performed? Who will you work with? How demanding is the job? What are the challenges? Chapter 1 of this book is designed to help you in this regard.
- Find out about educational requirements and schooling expectations. Will you be able to meet any rigorous requirements? This chapter and chapter 3 will help you understand the educational paths and certification requirements.
- Seek out opportunities to volunteer or shadow professionals doing the job. Use your critical thinking skills to ask questions and consider

whether this is the right environment for you. This chapter also discusses ways to find internships, summer jobs, and other job-related experiences.

- Look into student aid, grants, scholarships, and other ways you can get help to pay for schooling. It's not just about student aid and scholarships, either. Some larger organizations will pay employees to go back to school to get further degrees.

- Build a timetable for taking requirement exams such as the SAT and ACT, applying to schools, visiting schools, and making your decision. You should write down all the important deadlines and have them at the ready when you need them.

- Continue to look for employment that matters during your college years—internships and work experiences that help you build hands-on experience and knowledge about your actual career.

- Find a mentor who is currently practicing in your field of interest. This person can be a great source of information, education, and connections. Don't expect a job (at least not at first); just build a relationship with someone who wants to pass along their wisdom and experience. Coffee meetings or even emails are a great way to start.

A mentor can help you figure out which way to go with your career aspirations.
SDI Productions/E +/Getty Images

WHERE TO GO FOR HELP

If you aren't sure where to start, your local library, school library, and guidance counselor office are great places to begin. Search your local or school library for resources about finding a career path and finding the right schooling that fits your needs and budget. Make an appointment with a counselor or email them and ask about taking career interest questionnaires. With a little prodding, you'll be directed to lots of good information online and elsewhere. You can start your research with these four sites:

- The Bureau of Labor Statistics' Career Outlook site at https://www.bls .gov/careeroutlook/home.htm. The US Department of Labor's Bureau of Labor Statistics site doesn't just track job statistics, as you learned in chapter 1. There is an entire portion of this site dedicated to young adults looking to uncover their interests and match those interests with jobs currently in the market. There is a section called "Career Planning for High Schoolers" that you should check out. Information is updated based on career trends and jobs in demand, so you'll get practice information as well.
- The Mapping Your Future site at https://www.mappingyourfuture.org/ helps you determine a career path and then helps you map out a plan to reach those goals. It includes tips on preparing for college, paying for college, job hunting, résumé writing, and more.
- The Education Planner site at http://www.educationplanner.org has separate sections for students, parents, and counselors. It breaks down the task of planning your career goals into simple, easy-to-understand steps. You can find personality assessments, get tips for preparing for school, learn from some Q&As from counselors, download and use a planner worksheet, read about how to finance your education, and more.
- TeenLife at https://www.teenlife.com/ calls itself "the leading source for college preparation" and it includes lots of information about summer programs, gap year programs, community service, and more. They believe that spending time out "in the world" outside of the classroom can help students do better in school, find a better fit in terms of career, and even interview better with colleges. This site contains lots of links to volunteer and summer programs.

Use these sites as jumping off points and don't be afraid to reach out to a real person, such as a guidance counselor, if you're feeling overwhelmed.

WHAT IF I DROPPED OUT OF HIGH SCHOOL?

In many ads for jobs, you'll see something like, "High school diploma or equivalent required." What does "equivalent" mean? Well, it means you passed the General Educational Development (GED) exam. Once you earn that credential, you can use it like a high school diploma to pursue further technical or vocational (or college) education and apply for jobs.

In most states you must be at least 16 years old to sit for the GED exam (in some states it's 18). The exam covers four topic areas: math, language arts, science, and social studies. The GED exam is now only administered on computer, so you need to at least know how to work a mouse and keyboard. Settle in, because completing the test usually takes all day.

You can register for the GED exam at www.ged.com. That website will also tell you everything you need to know about taking the exam, including when and where you can take it and any fees you'll need to pay.

Tip: Young adults with disabilities can face additional challenges when planning a career path. DO-IT (Disabilities, Opportunities, Internetworking, and Technology) is an organization dedicated to promoting career and education inclusion for everyone. Its website (https://www.washington.edu/doit/) contains a wealth of information and tools to help all young people plan a career path, including self-assessment tests and career exploration questionnaires.

AARON FOX: CT TECHNOLOGIST

Aaron Fox graduated with an associate degree in applied science through the radiology program at Columbus Regional Health in Columbus, Indiana. He has worked as an X-ray and CT technologist in the Radiology Department at Columbus Regional Health for the last 18 years.

Can you explain how you became interested in a career as a medical technician?

I had a hard time deciding what career path to choose after I got out of high school. A simple conversation about possible career choices with a family member started my potential interest in radiology. Sometime after that conversation, I ended up having a scan done for health reasons. I was able to talk to the radiology technologist about their job. That person's enjoyment of their job further sparked my interest in radiology. I took a few medical and anatomy classes in college and enjoyed them. My mind was made up; I decided I would pursue a career in radiology.

Can you talk about your current position? What do you do, day to day?

My official job title is a CT technologist. I have several job responsibilities that go along with that title. The long answer is that I perform CT exams, document symptoms and medical history for the radiology exam to the radiologist, coordinate the CT patient schedule, order supplies, answer phone calls, start IVs, clean and stock radiology rooms, transport patients, process 3D CT images, communicate with physicians, and more. The short answer is, I am simply one part of a group of medical professionals, and our goal is to take very good care of our patients. That is what we do. That is what I do.

Do you think education prepared you for your job? How so?

Yes, it did. I went through a radiology school program at Columbus Regional Hospital. That involved a mixture of learning in the classroom and hands-on experience in the radiology department. Under tech supervision, I got to perform several radiology procedures during my education. This on-the-job training was invaluable. It definitely was a great preparation for my job. It allowed me to develop the skills I needed and smoothly transition from being a student to a technologist.

What's the best part of your job?

Two things come to mind. Both are equally important. One is the positive feedback from patients—both verbal and nonverbal. Sometimes it's just a smile from a patient that helps me know we took great care of them. The second thing I like about my job is my coworkers. I get to work with a lot of great people. You spend a lot of time with them and they become like your family.

What's the most surprising thing about your job?

It may not be surprising, but it's amazing that I never stop learning. I feel like I'm still learning new things that make me a better radiology tech.

What are some characteristics of a good med tech?

A good attitude and a hard work ethic will get you far in most professions, and this one is no different. It's also good to have a desire to want to help people.

What advice do you have for young people considering this career?

My advice for those considering this career would be to job shadow, volunteer, and/or work in a medical facility. This is a great way to see if it's a career you would like to continue to pursue. It's also good to talk with people in the medical field and ask them questions you might have.

How can a young person prepare for this career while in high school?

Again, a great way to prepare for this career while in high school would be to job shadow, volunteer, and/or work in a medical facility. There are medical jobs that don't require a degree, such as a radiology tech assistant. This is a great way to be a part of a radiology team and see if radiology is a career choice you would like to pursue. It's also a great idea to speak to someone about classes you would need to pursue a radiology career. One resource would be your school counselor/advisor. Another resource is Columbus Regional Health, which has a radiology school program. Information is available on the Columbus Regional Health website at https://www.crh.org/.

Making High School Count

If you are interested in working in some capacity as a medical technician, there are some basic yet important things you can do while in high school to position yourself in the most advantageous way. Remember—it's not just about having the best application—it's also about figuring out what professions you actually would enjoy doing and which ones don't suit you.

- Load up on the sciences, especially biology and anatomy. A head start in anatomy, biology, and/or physiology will be a big help.
- Be comfortable using all kinds of computer software.
- Learn first aid and CPR. You'll need these important skills regardless of your profession.
- Hone your communication skills in English, speech, and debate. You'll need them to speak with everyone from doctors to patients to other coworkers.
- Volunteer in as many settings as you can. Read on to learn more about this important aspect of career planning.

Educational Requirements

There are three main levels of education that you can obtain, after earning your high school diploma—there is a four-year program in medical technology (or related field) for medical technologists, a two-year program in medical technology (or related field) for medical technicians, and a nondegree earning program (a certification process, which usually takes about a year), which also prepares you to be a medical technician. After finishing their schooling, technologists and technicians alike usually have to pass an exam and then must become licensed or certified, but this does depend on the state in which you work.[1]

FINDING AN ACCREDITED SCHOOL

Regardless of whether you pursue the associate (two-year) degree, bachelor's (four-year) degree, or a certification, it's important that the school or college you attend be recognized and accredited by the Commission on Accreditation of Allied Health Education Programs (CAAHEP).

Note: Keep in mind that community colleges and technical schools can be a much cheaper way (as much as half the cost) to attain the same degree/certification, and as long as those programs are accredited, it won't matter to potential employers that you didn't attend a more well-known university.

Hospital-sponsored degree programs are also great options as long as they are accredited—you take all your courses and do your clinical work (hands-on practice) through a specific hospital. Chapter 3 discusses this option in more detail.

CLASSES YOU'LL TAKE

Regardless of the program you pursue, some of the typical classes you would take include the following:

- Basic biology
- Biotechnology
- Introduction to medical terminology
- Basic anatomy and physiology

- Communication skills for health care
- Clinical chemistry
- Medical lab procedures
- Immunology

Remember, if you are interested in becoming a medical technologist or technician and are still in middle or high school, you should take classes in biology and other sciences, as well as math.

CHOOSING THE RIGHT EDUCATION FOR YOU

You have three educational options to become a med tech—a non-degree certification (about one year), which includes most hospital-sponsored degree programs, an associate degree (about two years), or a bachelor's degree (about four years). The first two will lead to you being a "medical technician," whereas the last one leads to the title of "medical technologist." The introduction and chapter 1 both discussed the difference between these titles.

The quickest way to start a career as a med tech is through the *nondegree certification courses*. These are good options if you don't have the time or money to attend school for two or more years and instead need or want to get out into the workforce as soon as possible. The drawback is that you will be limited in upward mobility due to your lack of education. However, many employers will pay for their employees to continue their education. You could very well get your certification, begin working in the field, then later be reimbursed by your employer for earning your associate or bachelor's degree. Once you earn your new degree, you'll be set for a promotion with more responsibility and more money! Although working full time and attending school is not easy, it can pay off nicely in the end.

Tip: Visit the Commission on Accreditation of Allied Health Education Programs (CAAHEP) website (https://www.caahep.org/) for an updated and complete list of med tech programs that have been accredited by the CAAHEP. The site provides links to each state so you can see the accredited programs in your area. This is a good place to start to find a school that's accredited *and* meets your educational and financial needs.

A particularly good option under the "nondegree certification" umbrella are hospital-sponsored degree programs. They are just as they sound—you take all your courses and do your clinical work (hands-on practice) through a specific hospital (or hospital system). If you want to work in a hospital setting, these can be very good and economical ways of becoming a medical technician. Because your training takes place at/in the hospital, you get more real-life training and educational opportunities. You could end up with considerably more hands-on experience with patients and technology than with comparable university offerings.

You'll also have more access to doctors, current research, and the opportunity to be in the hub of best practice and patient care. Perhaps the best benefit to such programs is that, in all likelihood, you'll have a job waiting for you once you finish the program and become certified.

As with any program, be sure that the hospital's program is accredited by the proper bodies and check out their graduation rates as well as the percentage of students that pass their certification exams (such as the ARRT—American Registry of Radiologic Technologists—certification). These are two important markers that show they offer a high-quality program. Of course, check out the reputation of the hospital too.

ASSOCIATE DEGREE OR BACHELOR'S DEGREE?

Although requirements vary by state and even by hospital, many areas of med tech require at least an associate degree. That generally includes cardiovascular technologists, nuclear medicine technologists, certain laboratory techs, and many areas of radiologic technology.[2]

If you have decided you want to obtain a degree rather than a certificate, you need to decide which option is best for your circumstances—an associate degree or a bachelor's degree.

- *Associate degree:* Taking about two years, full time, to finish, these degrees are less expensive and less time consuming, and will have you joining the workforce sooner. In many cases, you can work with your associate degree, but it is also transferable to a bachelor's degree if you decide that's your next step.
- *Bachelor's degree:* Taking about two additional years, full time, to finish, these degrees give you a more comprehensive education, which may translate into greater job opportunities and growth (think management

and leadership). You'll be qualified to work in a broader range of medical settings than the person holding an associate degree.

There is no one right answer here. The best course of action is to determine what's required in the area of medical technology that you're most interested in. Some require more education than others, and you don't want to be caught unaware. The best education for you is one that you can afford, that gets you the education you need to break into the field, and that arms you with skills that are marketable. For one person, that may be certification, whereas for another it's a bachelor's degree in medical technology.

GETTING CERTIFIED

Recall that a *person* is certified, whereas a *school* is accredited (see the sidebar on the following page). Although each state regulates medical technologists and technicians differently, it's a good idea to get certified in the area of med tech that you want to work in—being certified will give you a leg up in finding a job and as well as being more prepared for the actual job.

Professional certifications are available from different agencies, depending on your specialty area:

- The American Registry for Diagnostic Medical Sonographers offers certifications for various areas of sonography, including breast, OB/GYN, cardiac, pediatrics, and more (http://www.ardms.org/Pages/default.aspx)
- Cardiovascular Credentialing International offers certifications such as Certified Cardiatric Technician, Registered Vascular Specialist, Certified Rhythm Analysis Technician, and more (http://www.cci-online.org/)
- American Registry of Radiologic Technologists offers 15 certifications, including bone densitometry (BD), radiation therapy (RT), computed tomography (CT), magnetic resonance imaging (MR), and vascular sonography (VS) (https://www.arrt.org/)
- The American Medical Technologists (AMT) offers various certifications for laboratory consultants, medical laboratory assistants, and molecular diagnostic technologists (https://americanmedtech.org/)
- The American Association of Medical Assistants (https://www.aama-ntl .org/) certifies people to become a Certified Medical Assistant (CMA)
- The American Registry of Radiologic Technologists (ARRT) certifies people operating medical imaging equipment (https://www.arrt.org/)

As you may have noticed, there is some credentialing overlap. It's best to determine which certifications are accepted/desired in your geographical area before you begin the certification process. For example, many states require med techs to earn certification from the American Registry of Radiologic Technologists (ARRT) in order to receive a state-issued license or permit to work with medical imaging equipment, while others view ARRT certification as sufficient on its own.[3]

WHAT'S THE DIFFERENCE BETWEEN ACCREDITATION AND CERTIFICATION?

These terms can be confusing and people often mess them up and use them incorrectly, contributing to the overall confusion. To clear it up, *accreditation* is the act of officially recognizing an organizational body, person, or educational facility as having a particular status or being qualified to perform a particular activity. For example, schools and colleges are accredited.

Certification, on the other hand, is the process of confirming that a person has certain skills or knowledge. This is usually provided by some third-party review, assessment, or educational body (in the case of med techs, this is usually handled by independent agencies). Individuals, not organizations, are certified. This also might be referred to as being *licensed* or *credentialed*.

Getting certified as a med tech puts you in a better position to find the job you want.
xavierarnau/E +/Getty Images

Experience-Related Requirements

It's important to realize that any health-care-related education you pursue—including medical technology and imaging—will require hours of clinical work, which includes hands-on practice with patients in real-world settings. The number of hours of clinical experience you need depends on the degree you pursue, as well as your own state's requirements. You might wonder how you can prepare for that experience and use fieldwork and/or internships to "test the waters," so to speak, so you can determine whether being a medical technician really is for you.

This section helps point you to ways in which you can gain critical experience in the field before and during the time you're pursuing your education. This can and should start in middle school or high school, especially during the summers. Experience is important for many reasons, not the least:

- Shadowing others in the profession can help reveal what the job is really like and whether it's something that you think you want to do, day in and day out. This is a relatively risk-free way to explore different career paths. Ask any "seasoned" adult and they will tell you that figuring out what you *don't* want to do is sometimes more important than figuring out what you *do* want to do.
- Internships and volunteer work are a relatively quick way to gain work experience and develop job skills.
- Volunteering can help you learn the intricacies of the profession, such as what types of environments are best, what kind of care fits you better, and which areas are in more demand.
- Gaining experience during your high school years sets you apart from the many others who are applying to programs.
- Volunteering in the field means that you'll be meeting many others doing the job that you might someday want to do (e.g., career networking). You have the potential to develop mentor relationships, cultivate future job prospects, and get to know people who can recommend you for later positions. Studies show that about 85 percent of jobs are found through personal contacts.[4]

Experience can come in the form of volunteering at the local clinic or hospital, taking on an internship in the summer, finding a summer job that complements your interests, or even attending camps that foster your career

"CT changes quickly. If you are in a hospital room setting, emergency room patients can be in critical condition and it's fast-paced. My day-to-day is varied and different depending on what's going on in the hospital. I find the hospital setting a little more interesting and exciting because you deal with trauma and it's different every day. I like the wide variety." —Heidi Bryant, CT technician

aspirations (see https://www.teenlife.com/ to start). Consider these tidbits of advice to maximize your volunteer experience.[5] They will help you stand out in competitive fields:

- Get diverse experiences. For example, try to shadow in at least two different medical settings.
- Try to gain four hours of volunteer experience in each setting. This is typically considered enough to show that you understand what a full workweek looks like in that setting. This can be as few as four to five hours per week over 10 weeks or so.
- If your profession has such a job, find an aide/tech position. Working as a paid aide is by far the best experience you can get. This will prepare you nicely for your clinical experiences and tests as well.
- Don't be afraid to ask questions. Just be considerate of the professionals' time and wait until they are not busy to pursue your questions. Asking good questions shows that you have a real curiosity for the profession.
- Maintain and cultivate professional relationships. Write thank-you notes, send updates about your application progress, tell them where you decide to go to school, and check in occasionally. If you want to find a good mentor, you need to be a gracious and willing mentee.

If you're currently in high school and you're seriously thinking about becoming a med tech, start by reaching out to a med tech who works at your local hospital, or to a family friend who works as a med tech. Start by asking good questions and showing your curiosity. Ask to shadow them if possible, remembering the guidelines about courtesy above. Don't expect to be paid for any of this effort. The benefit of volunteering is that it's much easier to get your foot in the door, but the drawback is that you typically will not be paid. However, with time and hard work, your volunteer position may turn into something else.

Look at these kinds of experiences as ways to learn about the profession, show people how capable you are, and make connections to others that could last your career. It may even help you to get into the program of your choice, and it will definitely help you write your personal statement as to why you want to be a med tech.

Another way to find a position is to start with your high school guidance counselor or website. Also visit the websites listed in this book and search the web for offices in your area. Don't be afraid to pick up the phone and call them. Be prepared to start by cleaning facilities, assisting staff with clerical work, and other such tasks. Being onsite, no matter what you're doing, will teach you more than you know. With a great attitude and work ethic, you will likely be given more responsibility over time. Once you are in your program, you will get many hours on hands-on experience as well.

STACEY BETTEGNIES: TEACHING RADIOGRAPHY

Stacey Bettegnies started her career in radiography in 1994. She graduated from X-ray school with an associate degree and worked as a CAT scan technologist for 25 years in the hospital setting, at Community Howard Hospital. She was the lead CAT scan technologist for 15 years. In 2013, she got her bachelor's degree, and in 2015, she got her master's degree. In 2015, she started teaching as an adjunct professor in the IUK (Indiana University-Kokomo) radiography program. In 2019, she became a full-time teacher.

She is currently the clinical coordinator and an assistant professor in the radiography program at IUK. She is in charge of placing students into their clinical studies rotations in hospitals. She also teaches physics for radiography students, principles of radiography, and medical terminology. She helps students in their clinical positions and ensures they are doing well.

Can you explain how you became interested in a career as a CT technician?

When I was in high school, I thought I was going to be an accountant. But then I decided I wanted to do something that would help people. I was in a car wreck my senior year in high school and I had a lot of X-rays and CAT scans during that time. I found it all fascinating. That changed my mind. I knew I wanted to do something in health care and that area was fascinating to me. I knew as soon as I got into school, I really liked it and knew I wanted to go into it.

Can you talk about your last job in the field? What was the best part of that job?

I still work PRN (which means she's called in as needed) at Community Howard and I really love the job. I love the people. Every day is different! That's great. You see trauma, and so on. It's all different and you are extremely busy. I like that. It keeps you busy and learning and the technology is always changing. It's great for your mind. You continue to learn. New pathology, diseases, trauma, and so on. It's a challenge. There's never a dull moment and it keeps you on your toes!

Can you talk about your current position as an educator?

I always knew I wanted to go back to school. There are lots of higher eds in my family. But I never thought I would teach. I decided to pursue my master's degree so I could go into management. I was asked to be an adjunct teacher, and I did it at first for the extra money. But I really enjoyed it. I loved to learn! I enjoy college, learning, writing papers, and so on. I love learning. By teaching, you learn from students. I also was able to give students knowledge from my experience. I loved helping students by sharing my years of experience. It went from a fun and rewarding experience to something I wanted to do full time. A position opened due to a retirement, and it was a big leap for me. I never thought in my mid-forties I would switch careers. But I really love watching the students when they first learn something or get an X-ray right the first time—it's amazing to see. In clinicals, they see what they learned in class and it clicks. That's fascinating to watch it click with students. I love giving back to this field and I do enjoy it. I had one semester and then COVID-19 hit. That's been a real struggle. I had to revamp everything I just started learning how to teach. We are trying to get back to somewhat normal again. We came back online last semester on campus since we are clinical, full time, still with some distance and mask restrictions.

Do you think your education prepared you for your job?

Yes, it did, but my experience working in the field gave me a lot of preparation as well. My background working as a technologist helped me be prepared to teach. I have a master's in public management, and bachelor's in medical imaging. I've had public health courses, which helped me go into clinical/hospital settings as well.

What's the best part of your current job?

As a teacher, the best part is the rewarding feeling I get from students when things click! When they succeed, I feel like I had a part in that and it feels great. People don't go into teaching for the money.

As far as being a CT technologist, the best part is knowing that you are helping someone. I deal with oncology patients and you see them on a routine basis. You bond with them and it feels good to be able to help them manage their health care.

CT is used in lots of trauma cases too, so you have a hand in helping patients and contribute to their medical care.

What about the profession do you find especially challenging?

Realizing that health care is a business, which is hard for me to swallow sometimes. Sometimes you are understaffed due to cost measures. You want to give the best patient care, and sometimes you are busting to get people in and out to make it profitable. You sometimes feel like you don't get to give them all the time they need and you feel like you are shortchanging them because you are rushing to get to the next patient who is waiting.

What are some characteristics of a good medical technician?

You need empathy and compassion, flexibility, creativity, and must be able to think out of the box. Not everything is a standard out-of-the-book case. You have to be flexible about what you might find, what patients need from you, emergencies that change your personal plans, and so forth. Your schedule might change and you have to be flexible. It's not always going to be cut and dried and black and white. You may have to stay over or go in early depending on cases coming in.

What advice do you have for young people considering this career?

Job shadow for sure. Spend some time in a department and see what they do. It's more than X-raying a bone. Make sure you don't have a problem with blood or bodily fluids, for example. You don't want to spend two years in school and then find out you can't handle the trauma cases! Investigate and research what they do and what happens on a day-to-day basis. Talk with some technologists and see what they say about their jobs—what they like and don't like.

How can a young person prepare for this career while in high school?

You can even job shadow as a high school student. Do some research on the internet. There are lots of videos and testimonials online, which can show you what the day-to-day experience is like.

Networking

Because it's so important, here's another word about networking. It's important to develop mentor relationships even at this stage. Remember that about

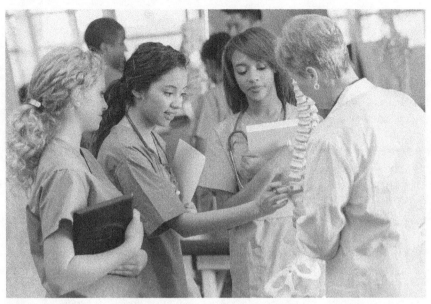

Volunteering and job shadowing are great ways to get real-world experience in health care.
SDI Productions/E +/Getty Images

85 percent of jobs are found through personal contacts. If you know someone in the field, don't hesitate to reach out. Be patient and polite, but ask for help, perspective, and guidance.

If you don't know anyone who is a med tech, ask your school guidance counselor to help you make connections, or pick up the phone yourself. Reaching out with a genuine interest in knowledge and a real curiosity about the field will go a long way. You don't need a job or an internship just yet—just a connection that could blossom into a mentoring relationship.

If you are stumped, take a minute to consider all the people you know. To begin with, you can probably count some or all of the following among your contacts right now:

- Parents
- Extended family members (aunts and uncles, cousins; perhaps grand-parents)
- Friends (plus their parents and older siblings)
- Social media friends (Instagram, Snapchat, Twitter, Facebook, etc.)
- Teachers

- School administrators
- Coaches, club leaders, and sponsors (band, student council, yearbook)
- Clergy (pastor, rabbi, imam, priest)
- Employers and former employers
- Coworkers and former coworkers
- Neighbors
- Fellow church or club members (people you know from church or local clubs like 4-H Club, Lion's Club, Elks and Moose lodges, or Knights of Columbus)

Suddenly it seems that you actually know quite a few people. Now, imagine how many people *they* know.

Now start writing down these contact names, phone numbers, and email addresses drawn in an address book of some kind. In many cases, you may only have a name. That's okay for now—write them down too. These single names can serve as placeholders until you get their phone numbers and email addresses.

Once you have a good number of contacts written down, come up with a short statement that says what kind of help you're looking for. For example, something like this:

> *Hi, _____. I'm looking for contacts in the _____ field as I consider my career choices. I am wondering if you might know someone I could talk to about this in order to expand my network as I look for information, training, and job shadowing opportunities. If you know of anyone who might be of help and you feel comfortable passing along their contact info, I would truly appreciate it!*

Save your statement in generic form and then paste it into emails, instant messages, or text messages and customize it as appropriate each time (*don't* forget to customize it). If you prefer speaking on the phone, prepare a similar brief appeal that you can deliver verbally. Be brief, but don't be shy. Most people are more than willing to help if they can. Try to contact 5 people like this per day. That's enough to start making progress on expanding your network, but it's not enough to be overwhelming or burdensome. In no time, your address book will be filling up. For example, by the end of the first week you will have contacted 35 people and may have collected some 35 new contacts.

Once you've made a new contact, use a similar script or speech with them, being sure to mention your common acquaintance by name. See if they are available to meet to discuss the career, training, and job opportunities you're interested in. If your meeting goes well, don't hesitate to ask if they know of someone else you may want to talk to.

Follow these important but simple rules for the best results when networking:

- Do your homework about a potential contact, connection, university, or employer before you make contact. Be sure to have a general understanding of what they do and why, but don't be a know-it-all. Be open and ready to ask good questions.
- Be considerate of professionals' time and resources. Think about what they can get from you in return for mentoring or helping you.
- Speak and write with standard, professional English. Proofread all your letters, emails, and even texts. Think about how you will be perceived at all times.
- Always stay positive.
- Show your passion for the subject matter.

Tip: Don't forget that your high school guidance counselor can be a great source of information and connections.

Summary

In this chapter, you learned even more about what it takes to become a med tech and the various education options you have. You also learned about getting experience in this field before you enter school as well as during the educational process. At this time, you should have a good idea of the educational requirements of the two areas you can pursue. You hopefully even contemplated some questions about what kind of educational career path fits your strengths, time requirements, and wallet. Are you starting to picture your career plan? If not, that's okay, as there's still time.

Remember that no matter which of these roles you pursue, you must maintain licensure and certifications and meet the continuing education requirements. Advances in understanding in the fields of health, medicine, nutrition, and more are continuous, and it's vitally important that you keep apprised of what's happening in your field. The bottom line is that you need to have a life-long love of learning to succeed in any health care field.

In chapter 3, we go into a lot more detail about pursuing the best educational path. The chapter covers the process of researching schools and finding the best fit for your needs, as well as how to find the best value for your education. The chapter includes a discussion about financial aid and scholarships. At the end of chapter 3, you should have a much clearer view of the educational landscape and how and where you fit in.

3

Pursuing the Educational Path

*W*hen it comes time to start looking at colleges, universities, or postsecondary schools, many high schoolers tend to freeze up at the enormity of the job ahead of them. This chapter will help break down this process for you so it won't seem so daunting.

Yes, finding the right college or learning institution is an important one, and it's a big step toward achieving your career goals and dreams. The last chapter covered the various educational requirements to be a med tech, which means you should now be ready to find the right institution of learning. This isn't always just a process of finding the very best school that you can afford and can be accepted into, although that might end up being your path. It should also be about finding the right fit so that you can have the best possible experience during your post–high school years.

Here's the truth of it all—attending postsecondary schooling isn't just about getting a degree. It's about learning how to be an adult, managing your life and your responsibilities, being exposed to new experiences, growing as a person, and otherwise moving toward becoming an adult who contributes to society. College offers you an opportunity to actually become an interesting person with perspective on the world and empathy and consideration for people other than yourself, if you let it.

An important component of how successful college will be for you is finding the right fit, the right school that brings out the best in you and challenges you at different levels. I know, no pressure, right? Just as with finding the right profession, your ultimate goal should be to match your personal interests/goals/personality with the college's goals and perspective. For example, small liberal arts colleges have a much different "feel" and philosophy than Big-10 or Pac-12 state schools. And rest assured that all this advice applies even when you're planning on attending community college or another postsecondary school.

WHAT IS A GAP YEAR?

Taking a year off between high school and college, often called a *gap year*, is normal, perfectly acceptable, and almost required in many countries around the world, and it is becoming increasingly acceptable in the United States as well. Even Malia Obama, former president Barack Obama's eldest daughter, did it. Because the cost of college has gone up dramatically, it literally pays for you to know going in what you want to study, and a gap year—well spent—can do lots to help you answer that question.

Some great ways to spend your gap year include joining the Peace Corps or AmeriCorps organizations, enrolling in a mountaineering program or other gap year–styled program, backpacking across Europe or other countries on the cheap (be safe and bring a friend), find a volunteer organization that furthers a cause you believe in or that complements your career aspirations, join a Road Scholar program (see www .roadscholar.org), teach English in another country (see https://www.gooverseas .com/blog/best-countries-for-seniors-to-teach-english-abroad for more informa-tion), or work and earn money for college!

Many students will find that they get much more out of college when they have a year to mature and to experience the real world. The American Gap Year Association reports from their alumni surveys that students who take gap years show improved civic engagement, improved college graduation rates, and improved GPAs in college.[1]

See their website at https://gapyearassociation.org/ for lots of advice and resources if you're considering a potentially life-altering experience.

Don't worry, though, in addition to these "soft skills," this chapter does dive into the nitty-gritty of finding the best schools, no matter what you want to do. In the health care field specifically, attending an accredited program is critical to future success, and we cover that in detail in this chapter.

Finding a School That's Right for You

Before you start your search in earnest, it will behoove you to take some time to consider what "type" of school will be best for you. If nothing else, answering questions like the following ones can help you narrow your search and focus on a smaller sampling of choices.

Community colleges, as long as they are accredited, can be great places of learning for a fraction of the cost.
martinedoucet/E +/Getty Images

Write your answers to these questions down somewhere where you can refer to them often, such as in your Notes app on your phone:

- *Size*: Does the size of the school matter to you? Colleges and universities range from sizes of 500 or fewer students to 40,000 students.
- *Community location:* Would you prefer to be in a rural area, a small town, a suburban area, or a large city? How important is the location of the school in the larger world to you?
- *Distance from home:* How far away from home do you want/are you willing to go? Phrase this in terms of hours away or miles away.
- *Housing options:* What kind of housing would you prefer and can you afford? Dorms, off-campus apartments, and private homes are all common options.
- *Student body:* How would you like the student body to "look"? Think about coed versus all-male and all-female settings, as well as the racial and ethnic diversity of the student body, how many students are part time versus full time, average age, and the percentage of commuter students.

- *Academic environment:* Consider which majors are offered and at which levels of degree. Research the student-faculty ratio. Are the classes taught often by actual professors or more often by the teaching assistants? Find out how many internships the school typically provides to students. Are independent study or study abroad programs available in your area of interest? And of course, do they offer the program or programs you are interested in?
- *Financial aid availability/cost:* Does the school provide ample opportunities for scholarships, grants, work-study programs, and the like? Does cost play a role in your options (for most people, it does)?
- *Support services:* Investigate the strength of the academic and career placement counseling services of the school.
- *Social activities and athletics:* Does the school offer clubs that you are interested in? Which sports are offered? Are scholarships available?
- *Specialized programs:* Does the school offer honors programs or programs for veterans or students with disabilities or special needs?

Not all of these questions are going to be important to you, and that's fine. Be sure to make note of aspects that don't matter so much to you too, such as size or location. You might change your mind as you go to visit colleges, but it's important to make note of how you feel at the beginning of your search.

CONSIDER THE SCHOOL'S REPUTATION

One factor in choosing a college or certificate program is the school's reputation. This reputation is based on the quality of education previous students have received there. If you go to a school with a healthy reputation in your field, it gives potential employers a place to start when they are considering your credentials and qualifications.

Factors vary depending on which schools offer the program you want, so take these somewhat lightly. Some of the factors affecting reputation generally include:

- *Nonprofit or for profit*—In general, schools that are nonprofit (or not-for-profit) organizations have better reputations than for-profit schools.

In fact, it's best to avoid for-profit schools. For one, the intensity of academic programs may be reduced to allow students with lower grades and abilities to keep up with courses.

- *Accreditation*—Your program must be accredited by a regional accrediting body to be taken seriously in the professional world. It would be very rare to find an unaccredited college or university with a good reputation.
- *Acceptance rate*—Schools that accept a very high percentage of applicants can have lower reputations than those that accept a smaller percentage. That's because a high acceptance rate can indicate that there isn't much competition for those spaces, or that standards are not as high.
- *Alumni*—What have graduates of the program gone on to do? The college's or department's website can give you an idea of what their graduates are doing.
- *History*—Schools that have been around a long time tend to be doing something right. They also tend to have good alumni networks, which can help you when you're looking for a job or a mentor.
- *Faculty*—Schools with a high percentage of permanent faculty vs. adjunct faculty tend to have better reputations. Bear in mind that if you're going to a specialized program or certification program, this might be reversed—these programs are frequently taught by experts who are working in the field.
- *Departments*—A department at one school might have a better reputation than a similar department at a school that's more highly ranked overall. If the *department* you'll be attending is well known and respected, that could be more important than the overall reputation of the institution itself.

AFTER THE RESEARCH, TRUST YOUR GUT

There are a lot of websites that claim to have the "Top Ten Schools for Medical Technicians" or "Best Twenty-Five Medical Imaging Programs." It's hard to tell which of those are truly accurate. So where do you begin? *US News & World Report* is a great place to start to find a college or university with a great reputation. Go to www.usnews.com/education to find links to the highest-ranked schools for the undergraduate or graduate degree programs you're interested in.

US News & World Report puts it best when they say the college that fits you best is one that will do all these things:

- Offers a degree that matches your interests and needs
- Provides a style of instruction that matches the way you like to learn
- Provides a level of academic rigor to match your aptitude and preparation
- Offers a community that feels like home to you
- Values you for what you do well[2]

Note: According to the National Center for Educational Statistics (NCES), which is part of the US Department of Education, six years after entering college for an undergraduate degree, only 59 percent of students have graduated.[3] Barely half of those students will graduate from college in their lifetime.[4]

As you look at the facts and figures, you also need to think about a less-quantifiable aspect of choosing a college or university: *fit*. What does that mean? It's hard to describe, but students know it when they feel it. It means finding the school that not only offers the program you want, but also the school that feels right. Many students have no idea what they're looking for in a school until they walk onto the campus for a visit. Suddenly, they'll say to themselves "This is the one!"

Hopefully, this section has impressed upon you the importance of finding the right college fit. Take some time to paint a mental picture about the kind of university or school setting that will best meet your needs.

Note: According to the US Department of Education,[5] as many as 32 percent of college students transfer colleges during the course of their educational career. This is to say that the decision you initially make is not set in stone. Do your best to make a good choice, but remember that you can change your mind, your major, and even your campus. Many students do it and go on to have great experiences and earn great degrees.

Honing Your Degree Plan

This section outlines the different approaches you can take to get a degree that will land you your dream job in medical technology, whether it be as an X-ray tech, CT tech, phlebotomist, or something else.

HOSPITAL-SPONSORED DEGREE PROGRAMS

Hospital-sponsored degree programs were explained in chapter 2. With these programs, you take all your courses and do your clinical work at a specific hospital. If you want to work in a hospital setting, these can be very good and economical ways of becoming a medical technician. You could end up with more hands-on experience with patients and technology than with comparable university offerings, and you'll likely have a job waiting at that hospital for you once you finish the program and become certified.

As mentioned in chapter 2, be sure that the hospital's program is accredited by the proper bodies and check out their graduation rates as well as the percentage of students that pass their certification exams.

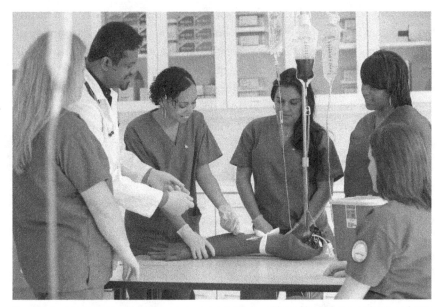

Hospital-sponsored degree programs can be a great way to get lots of hands-on experience and earn your degree quickly.
Ariel Skelley/DigitalVision/Getty Images

HOW IMPORTANT IS ACCREDITATION?

Accreditation is the process of ensuring that an academic program meets the common standards of quality set forth for that particular profession. Keep in mind that most companies will only hire people who received their degrees from a program that is accredited. This is especially true in the health-related fields, which are more heavily regulated. When you research a school or program, make sure you can verify that the program of study is accredited through the proper accreditation body.

Specifically with medical technicians, employers typically prefer (and many require) graduates of programs accredited by the Commission on Accreditation of Allied Health Education Programs (CAAHEP)—see *www.caahep.org*.

Researching Schools

If you're currently in high school and are serious about pursuing a career as a medical technician, whether that's through a hospital-sponsored degree program, an associate degree, or a bachelor's degree, start by finding four to five educational options in a realistic location (for you) that offer the degree/certificate/program in question. Not every school near you or that you have an initial interest in will probably offer the program you want of course, so narrow your choices accordingly. With that said, consider attending a university in your resident state, if possible, which will save you lots of money. Private institutions don't typically discount resident student tuition costs.

Be sure you research the basic GPA and SAT or ACT requirements of each school as well.

Once you have found four to five options in a realistic location for you that offer the degree/certificate in question (and are accredited), spend some time on their websites studying the requirements for admissions. Most universities will list the average stats for the last class accepted to the program. Important factors weighing on your decision of what schools to apply to should include whether or not you meet the requirements, your chances of getting in (shoot high!), tuition costs and availability of scholarships and grants, location, and the school's reputation and licensure/graduation rates. And of course, make sure they are accredited.

Note: For those of you applying to associate degree programs or greater, most advisors recommend that students take both the ACT and the SAT tests during their junior year (spring at the latest). (The ACT test is generally considered more weighted in science, so it may be more important if you plan on working in health care.) You can retake these tests and use your highest score, so be sure to leave time to retake early senior year if needed. You want your best score to be available to all the schools you're applying to by January of your senior year, which will also enable them to be considered with any scholarship applications. Keep in mind these are general timelines—be sure to check the exact deadlines and calendars of the schools to which you're applying!

"I went through a radiology school program at [my local hospital]. It involved a mixture of learning in the classroom and hands-on experience in the radiology department. Under supervision, I got to perform several radiology procedures. This on-the-job training was invaluable. It definitely was great preparation for my job. It allowed me to develop the skills I needed and smoothly transition from being a student to a technologist." —Aaron Fox, CT technologist

The order of these characteristics will depend on your grades and test scores, your financial resources, and other personal factors. You, of course, want to find a university (or hospital program) that has a good reputation for the science and health fields, but it's also important to match your academic rigor and practical needs with the best school you can.

Applying and Getting Admitted

Once you've narrowed down your list of potential schools, of course you'll want to be accepted. First, you need to apply.

There isn't enough room in this book to include everything you need to know about applying to colleges, but here is some useful information to get you started. Remember, every college and university is unique, so be sure to be in touch with their admissions offices so you don't miss any special requirements or deadlines.

Follow the guidelines here to get to "yes" and get admitted.
eyecrave/E +/Getty Images

It's a good idea to make yourself a "to-do" list while you're a junior in high school. Already a senior? Already graduated? No problem. It's never too late to start.

MAKE THE MOST OF SCHOOL VISITS

If it's at all practical and feasible, you should visit the schools you're considering (or the hospitals if you're considering a hospital-sponsored degree program). To get a real feel for any college or school, you need to walk around the campus and buildings, spend some time in the common areas where students hang out, and sit in on a few classes. You can also sign up for campus tours, which are typically given by current students. This is another good way to see the school and ask questions of someone who knows. Be sure to visit the specific school/building that covers your possible major as well. The website and brochures won't be able to convey that intangible feeling you'll get from a visit.

In addition to the questions listed in the previous section in this chapter entitled "Finding a School That's Right for You," consider these questions as well. Make a list of questions that are important to you before you visit.

- What is the makeup of the current freshman class? Is the campus diverse?
- What is the meal plan like? What are the food options?
- Where do most of the students hang out between classes? (Be sure to visit this area.)
- How long does it take to walk from one end of the campus to the other?
- What types of transportation are available for students? Does campus security provide escorts to cars, dorms, and so forth at night?

In order to be ready for your visit and make the most of it, consider these tips and words of advice.

Before you go,

- Be sure to do some research. At the least, spend some time on the college website. Make sure your questions aren't addressed adequately there first.
- Make a list of questions.
- Arrange to meet with a professor in your area of interest or to visit the specific school.
- Be prepared to answer questions about yourself and why you are interested in this school.

During the visit:

- Dress in neat, clean, and casual clothes. Avoid overly wrinkled clothing or anything with stains.
- Listen and take notes.
- Be positive and energetic.
- Make eye contact when someone speaks directly to you.
- Ask questions.

Finally, be sure to send thank-you notes or emails after the visit is over. Remind the recipient when you visited the campus and thank them for their time.

STANDARDIZED TESTS

Many colleges and universities require scores from standardized tests that are supposed to measure your readiness for college and ability to succeed. As you can read in the sidebar below, fewer and fewer colleges are requiring these standardized tests. For one, there is debate about how accurate these tests are, so some institutions don't ask for them anymore.

Assuming you decide to take these tests, let's take a look at them. To apply to an undergraduate program, students generally take either the SAT or the ACT. Both cover reading, writing, and math. Both have optional essays. Both

THE SAT IS OPTIONAL: SHOULD I TAKE IT ANYWAY?

More than half of four-year colleges and universities in the United States[6]—a staggering percentage—decided to make entrance exams like the SAT and ACT optional in 2021, and this is a change that may sustain for a lot longer. The main reason is to offer a more equitable approach when it comes to considering applicants, as SAT/ACT scores often do not accurately reflect a student's academic background.

What exactly does "test optional" mean? It varies from school to school. Be sure you know what it means for any school you are considering applying to. It can mean the following:

- Truly "test optional" means you decide if you want to submit your test scores. If you do, the scores will be taken into consideration along with other parts of the application. This implies that the test scores may carry less weight when compared with the other application elements, but will be considered.
- "Test flexible" schools will allow you to submit scores for the SAT or ACT, or a different test in their place (such as a SAT subject test or AP test).
- "Test blind" schools will not consider any scores, even if you include them in the application.

If you feel confident that your scores will be an asset to your application, then by all means take the test and submit the score. It will not hurt your chances and can only help them. If you take the test and are not satisfied that the results will give your application a positive edge, then you are not obligated to submit the scores. You really can't lose by preparing for and taking the tests.

are accepted by colleges and universities. Both take nearly the same amount of time to complete. If one test is preferred over another by schools, it's usually more about where you live than about the test.[7]

- *SAT*—Offered by the CollegeBoard.org. There are twenty SAT subject tests that you can take to show knowledge of special areas, such as math 1 and math 2, biology (ecological or molecular), chemistry, physics, as well as US or world history and numerous languages.
- *ACT*—Offered by ACT.org. There aren't any subject tests available with the ACT. Questions are a little easier on the ACT, but you don't have as much time to answer them.

Ultimately, which test you take comes down to personal preference. Many students choose to take both exams.

KNOW THE DEADLINES

- Early decision (ED) deadlines are usually in November, with acceptance decisions announced in December. Note that if you apply for ED admission and are accepted, that decision is usually binding, so only apply ED if you know exactly which school you want to go to and are ready to commit.
- ED II is a second round of early decision admissions. Not every school that does ED will also have an ED II. For those that do, deadlines are usually in January with decisions announced in February.
- Regular decision deadlines can be as early as January 1 but can go later. Decision announcements usually come out between mid-March and early April.
- Rolling admission is used by some schools. Applications are accepted at any time, and decisions are announced on a regular schedule. Once the incoming class is full, admissions for that year will close.

THE COMMON APP

The Common Application (Common App) form is a single, detailed application form that is accepted by more than 900 colleges and universities in the United States.[8] Instead of filling out a different application form for every school you want to apply to, you fill out one form and have it sent to all the schools you're interested in. The Common App itself is free, and most schools don't charge for submitting it.

If you don't want to use the Common App for some reason, most colleges will also let you apply with a form on their website. There are a few institutions that only want you to apply through their sites and other highly regarded institutions that only accept the Common App. Be sure you know the preferences of the schools you're interested in.

The Common App's website (www.commonapp.org) has a lot of useful information, including tips for first-time applicants and for transfer students.

ESSAYS

Part of any college application is a written essay, sometimes even two or three. Some colleges provide writing prompts they want you to address. The Common App has numerous prompts that you can choose from. Here are some issues to consider when writing your essays:

- *Topic*—Choose something that has some meaning for you and that you can speak to in a personal way. This is your chance to show the college or university who you are as an individual. It doesn't have to be about an achievement or success, and it shouldn't be your whole life story. Maybe a topic relates to a time you learned something or had an insight into yourself.
- *Timing*—Start working on your essays the summer before senior year, if possible. You won't have a lot of other homework in your way, and you'll have time to prepare thoughtful comments and polish your final essay.
- *Length*—Aim for between 250 and 650 words. The Common App leans toward the long end of that range, while individual colleges might lean toward the shorter end.
- *Writing*—Use straightforward language. Don't turn in your first draft. Work on your essay and improve it as you go. Ask someone else to read it and tell you what they think. Ask your English teacher to look at it and make suggestions. Do *not* let someone else write any portion of your essay. It needs to be *your* ideas and *your* writing in order to represent *you*.

- *Proofing*—Make sure your essay doesn't have any obvious errors. Run spell check, but don't trust it to find everything (spell checkers are notorious for introducing weird errors). Have someone you trust read it over for you and note spelling, grammar, and other mistakes. Nobody can proofread their own work and find every mistake—what you'll see is what you expect to see. Even professional editors need other people to proofread their writing! So don't be embarrassed to ask for help.

LETTERS OF RECOMMENDATION

Most college applications ask for letters of recommendation from people who know you well and can speak to what you're like as a student and as a person. How many you need varies from school to school, so check with the admissions office website to see what they want. Some schools don't want any!

Who Should You Ask for a Letter?

Some schools will tell you pretty specifically whom they want to hear from. Others leave it up to you. Choose people who know you and think well of you. Here are some possibilities:

- One or two teachers of your best academic subjects (math, science, social studies, etc.)
- Teacher of your best elective subject (art, music, media, etc.)
- Advisor for a club you're active in
- School counselor
- School principal (but only if you've taken a class with them or they know you individually as a student)
- Community member you've worked with, such as a scout leader, volunteer group leader, or religious leader
- Boss at a job you've held

When Should You Ask for a Letter?

Don't wait until applications are due. Give people plenty of time to prepare a good recommendation letter for you. If possible, ask for these letters in late spring or early summer of your junior year.

Submitting Your Letters of Recommendation

Technically, you're not supposed to read your recommendation letters. That lets recommenders speak more freely about you. Some might show you the letter anyway, but that's up to them. Don't ask to see it!

Recommenders can submit their letters electronically either directly to the institutions you're applying to or through the Common App. Your job is to be sure they know the submission deadlines well in advance so they can send in the letters on time.

Admissions Requirements

Each college or university will have their own admissions requirements. In addition, the specific program or major you want to go into may have admissions requirements of their own, in addition to the institution's requirements.

It's your responsibility to go to each institution's website and be sure you know and understand their requirements. That includes checking out each department site, too, to find any special prerequisites or other things that they're looking for.

THE MOST PERSONAL OF PERSONAL STATEMENTS

The *personal statement* you include with your application to college is extremely important, especially when your GPA is on the border of what is typically accepted. Write something that is thoughtful and conveys your understanding of the health care profession, as well as your desire to practice in this field. Why are you uniquely qualified? Why are you a good fit for this university? These essays should be highly personal (the "personal" in personal statement). Will the admissions professionals who read it, along with hundreds of others, come away with a snapshot of who you really are and what you are passionate about?

Look online for some examples of good ones, which will give you a feel for what works. Be sure to check your specific school for length guidelines, format requirements, and any other guidelines they expect you to follow.

And of course, be sure to proofread it several times and ask a professional (such as your school writing center or your local library services) to proofread it as well.

What's It Going to Cost You?

So, the bottom line is this: What will your education end up costing you? Of course, that depends on many factors, including the type and length of degree, where you attend (in-state or not, private or public institution), how much in scholarships or financial aid you're able to obtain, your family or personal income, and many other factors.

> "College may seem expensive. But the truth is that most students pay less than their college's sticker price, or published price, thanks to financial aid. So instead of looking at the published price, concentrate on your net price—the real price you'll pay for a college. . . . Your net price is a college's sticker price for tuition and fees minus the grants, scholarships, and education tax benefits you receive. The net price you pay for a particular college is specific to you because it's based on your personal circumstances and the college's financial aid policies." —BigFuture[9]

The College Entrance Examination Board (see www.collegeboard.org) tracks and summarizes financial data from colleges and universities all over the United States. A sample of data from the 2019–2020 academic year is shown in the following tables.

Table 3.1 shows the average estimated annual costs depending on the degree level you are pursuing. Table 3.2 shows undergraduate costs depending on the type of university. In both cases, costs shown are for one year.

Table 3.1.   Average Estimated Annual Costs by Degree Type, 2019–2020[10]

Sector	Undergraduate Degree Total (tuition, fees, room, and board)	Master's Degree Total (tuition, fees, room, and board)	Doctoral Degree Total (tuition, fees, room, and board)	Average Percent Increase in One Year
Private nonprofit four-year college	$48,380	$43,380	$60,160	3.3%
Public four-year college	$19,460	$19,570	$23,370	2.7%

Notes: Other expense categories, such as books, supplies, and transportation, are not included here.

Sources: College Board, Annual Survey of Colleges; NCES, IPEDS Fall 2019 Enrollment data and IPEDS 2018 Institutional Characteristics data.

Table 3.2. Average Estimated Annual Costs by Sector, 2009–2011.[11]

Sector	Tuition and Fees	Room and Board	Total	Average Percent Increase in One Year
Private nonprofit four-year college	$36,880	$12,990	$49,870	3.4%
Public four-year out-of-state college	$26,820	$11,510	$38,330	2.4%
Public four-year in-state college	$10,440	$11,510	$21,950	2.3%
Public two-year in-district college	$3,730	$8,990	$12,720	2.8%

Notes: Other expense categories, such as books, supplies, and transportation, are not included here.

Sources: College Board, Annual Survey of Colleges; NCES, IPEDS Fall 2019 Enrollment data and IPEDS 2018 Institutional Characteristics data.

Keep in mind these are averages and reflect the *published* prices, not the net prices. As an example of net cost, in 2019–2020, full-time in-state students at public four-year colleges must cover an average of about $15,400 in tuition and fees and room and board after grant aid and tax benefits, in addition to paying for books and supplies and other living expenses.[12]

If you read more specific data about a particular university or find averages in your particular area of interest, you should assume those numbers are closer to reality than these averages, as they are more specific. This data helps to show you the ballpark figures.

Generally speaking, there is about a 3 percent annual increase in tuition and associated costs to attend college. In other words, if you are expecting to attend college two years after this data was collected, you need to add approximately 6 percent to these numbers. Keep in mind again that this assumes no financial aid or scholarships of any kind (so it's not the net cost).

STACIA MELLINGER

Stacia Mellinger originally got her bachelor's degree in English literature and worked in publishing for about 15 years. She wanted to get out from behind a computer and do something with more face-to-face interaction and physical activity.

"I looked at nursing, and so forth, and I really liked the X-ray tech idea. I did research, got my pre-recs [prerequisites], and decided on the hospital program at Columbus Regional Hospital. I graduated as a radiological technologist and

Stacia Mellinger.
Courtesy of Stacia Mellinger.

stayed on. I have been there for about 10 years now. I am essentially an X-ray tech."

Can you explain how you became interested in a career as an X-ray technician?

My dad was a doctor, and my mom was an X-ray tech. When I was younger, I rebelled against the idea of health care. I did enjoy my first career in publishing, but when it was time for a change, I came back around to the health care idea. I liked the idea of being an X-ray tech because it seemed like a perfect combination of patient care, technology, and medicine.

Can you talk about your current position? What do you do, day to day?

I take care of people—that's the number one thing in my mind. When I am training other techs, that's the first thing I tell them. It's our job to take care of people. Patients often come to us feeling vulnerable. I play a part in their health care in terms of diagnosing issues. Patients come in with a need for diagnostics, such as for pathology. The majority of my time is spent in the ER—for injuries, heart attacks, stroke, accidents, and so on, and we need to imagine them. I help the docs determine what steps need to be taken for the patient's health.

I also spend a lot of time in surgery. I do the imaging so there is less actual cutting and the operation can be less invasive. I do imaging as the surgery is happening.

Scheduled patients usually involve chest X-rays for possible pneumonia, pre-op testing, unidentified symptoms (due to COVID-19 for example). I do basic X-rays, chest X-rays, broken bones, cancer masses, and so on.

In the ER, for example, a coded person may have stopped breathing—could be an overdose, heart attack, or something else. In the ER, they are intubated, breathing is stabilized, blood is drawn. This is all happening at once. I also have to get a chest X-ray to make sure the intubation tube is in the lungs and not in the stomach, for example. There are lots of people in the room. We put our board under the back and take a picture to make sure the tube is placed correctly. We do this as quickly and efficiently as possible because the doctors and nurses have to step out while we do this. It gets a little hairy and the pressure is on to get out of the way so the doctors and others can get back in the room.

Even so, I never feel stress there. I am well trained and I know what to do. I feel ready and prepared. I am part of a team of professionals.

Do you think your education prepared you for your job?

Yes. My education was a great combo of classroom and clinical work. About 60 percent was clinical. The classroom time is important, but the clinical aspect is critical. You work for two years doing the job while someone is holding your hand, essentially. So, once you graduate, you are set to go. You feel pretty prepared by that time.

What's the best part of your job?

My favorite part is interacting with the patients and meeting new people every day. I love trying to find out what they need—whether they need me to be quiet, compassionate, jokey, calm, and so on. People are awesome. I love interacting with them. I never thought I would be that kind of person. Anyone can learn the technical part of my job, but to be able to figure out what patients need emotionally and give that to them is rewarding. I feel I am good at that part too. It's very gratifying.

I know what to do and can do it well. That's gratifying. I don't like gray areas really. I do have to think out of the box but can have different ways to get there, but it all leads to the same task, and I can do that task well.

What about your profession do you find especially challenging?

There are people in management positions that sometimes make decisions about our day-to-day jobs and determine what we do who don't work with patients and don't do our jobs. Those decisions sometimes seem to be motivated by money instead of patient care. I understand that they do need to consider the financial health of the hospital, but it can be hard when you're on the patient end of things.

What are some characteristics of a good X-ray technician?

Compassion for sure. Flexibility is important, as well as ingenuity. It also requires a lot of energy. I get pulled in many different directions, such as when there's an emergency or an issue in surgery. You'll be pulled in different directions and you need to roll with it.

You often have to think outside the box to use the equipment and give radiology the best picture but also work with the patient, who may be injured and in pain.

What advice do you have for young people considering this career?

First, do it. It's awesome, and I love it. You have to really enjoy people, otherwise you won't be good and won't enjoy it. It's hard work, so be ready for that.

How can a young person prepare for this career while in high school?

Job shadow, like at a hospital. Talk to people who do it. Also, be sure to focus on the hard sciences while in high school. There's lots of physics and math.

Financial Aid and Student Loans

Finding the money to attend college, whether it is two or four years, a hospital program, or a vocational career college, can seem overwhelming, but you can do it if you have a plan before you actually start applying to college. If you get into your top-choice university, don't let the sticker cost turn you away. Financial aid can come from many different sources, and it's available to cover all different kinds of costs you'll encounter during your years in college, including tuition, fees, books, housing, and food.

The good news is that universities more often offer incentive or tuition discount aid to encourage students to attend. The market is often more competitive in the favor of the student and colleges and universities are responding by offering more generous aid packages to a wider range of students than they used to. Here are some basic tips and pointers about the financial aid process:

- You apply for financial aid during your senior year. You must fill out the FAFSA (Free Application for Federal Student Aid) form, which can be

NOT ALL FINANCIAL AID IS CREATED EQUAL

Educational institutions tend to define financial aid as any scholarship, grant, loan, or paid employment that assists students to pay their college expenses. Notice that "financial aid" covers both *money you have to pay back* and *money you don't have to pay back.* That's a big difference!

DO NOT HAVE TO BE REPAID

- Scholarships
- Grants
- Work study

HAVE TO BE REPAID *WITH INTEREST*

- Federal government loans
- Private loans
- Institutional loans

filed starting October 1 of your high school senior year until June of the year you graduate.[13] Because the amount of available aid is limited, it's best to apply as soon as you possibly can. See fafsa.gov to get started.

- Be sure to compare and contrast deals you get at different schools. There is room to negotiate with universities. The first offer for aid may not be the best you'll get.
- Wait until you receive all offers from your top schools and then use this information to negotiate with your top choice to see if they will match or beat the best aid package you received.
- To be eligible to keep and maintain your financial aid package, you must meet certain grade/GPA requirements. Be sure you are very clear on these academic expectations and keep up with them.
- You must reapply for federal aid every year.

Note: Watch out for scholarship scams! You should never be asked to pay to submit the FAFSA form ("free" is in its name) or be required to pay a lot to find appropriate aid and scholarships. These are free services. If an organization promises you that you'll get aid or that you have to "act now or miss out," these are both warning signs of a less reputable organization.

Also, be careful with your personal information to avoid identity theft as well. Simple things like closing and exiting your browser after visiting sites where you entered personal information (like fafsa.gov) goes a long way. Don't share your student aid ID number with anyone either.

It's important to understand the different forms of financial aid that are available to you. That way, you'll know how to apply for different kinds and get the best financial aid package that fits your needs and strengths. The two main categories that financial aid falls under are *gift aid,* which doesn't have to be repaid, and *self-help aid,* which are either loans that must be repaid or work-study funds that are earned. The next sections cover the various types of financial aid that fit in one of these areas.

GRANTS

Grants typically are awarded to students who have financial needs but can also be used in the areas of athletics, academics, demographics, veteran support, and special talents. They do not have to be paid back. Grants can come from federal agencies, state agencies, specific universities, and private organizations. Most federal and state grants are based on financial need.

Examples of grants are the Pell Grant, the SMART Grant, and the Army Corps Grant. Some of these federal grants are for health care professionals who are willing to work in less-served areas. For example, if you're willing to work in states or communities that have been traditionally underserved with health care services (including Indian reservations), you can receive federal grants and benefits.

SCHOLARSHIPS

Scholarships are merit-based aid that does not have to be paid back. They are typically awarded based on academic excellence or some other special talent, such as music or art. Scholarships also fall under the areas of athletic based, minority based, aid for women, and so forth. These are typically not awarded by federal or state governments, but instead, they come from the specific school you applied to as well as private and nonprofit organizations.

Paying for college can take a creative mix of grants, scholarships, and loans, but you can find your way with some help!
Casper1774Studio/iStock/Getty Images

Be sure to reach out directly to the financial aid officers of the schools you want to attend. These people are great contacts that can lead you to many more sources of scholarships and financial aid. Visit http://www.gocollege.com /financial-aid/scholarships/types/ for lots more information about how scholarships in general work.

LOANS

Many types of loans are available especially to students to pay for their postsecondary education. However, the important thing to remember here is that loans must be paid back, with interest. Be sure you understand the interest rate you will be charged. This is the extra cost of borrowing the money and is usually a percentage of the amount you borrow. Is this fixed or will it change over time? Is the loan and interest deferred until you graduate (meaning you don't have to begin paying it off until after you graduate)? Is the loan subsidized (meaning the federal government pays the interest until you graduate)? These are all points you need to be clear about before you sign on the dotted line.

There are many types of loans offered to students, including need-based loans, non-need-based loans, state loans, and private loans. Two very reputable federal loans are the Perkins Loan and the Direct Stafford Loan. For more information about student loans, start at https://bigfuture.collegeboard.org /pay-for-college/loans/types-of-college-loans.

FEDERAL WORK-STUDY

The US federal work-study program provides part-time jobs for undergraduate and graduate students with financial need so they can earn money to pay for educational expenses. The focus of such work is on community service work and work related to a student's course of study. Not all schools participate in this program, so be sure to check with the school financial aid office if this is something you are counting on. The sooner you apply, the more likely you will get the job you desire and be able to benefit from the program, as funds are limited. See https://studentaid.ed.gov/sa/types/work-study for more information about this opportunity.

Making High School Count

If you are still in high school or middle school, there are still many things you can do now to help the postsecondary educational process go more smoothly. Consider these tips for your remaining years:

- Work on listening well and speaking and communicating clearly. Work on writing clearly and effectively.
- Learn how to learn. This means keeping an open mind, asking questions, asking for help when you need it, taking good notes, and doing your homework.
- Plan a daily homework schedule and keep up with it. Have a consistent, quiet place to study.
- Talk about your career interests with friends, family, and counselors. They may have connections to people in your community who you can shadow or will mentor you.
- Try new interests or activities, especially during your first two years of high school.
- Be involved in extracurricular activities that truly interest you and say something about who you are and want to be.

Kids are under so much pressure these days to "do it all," but you should think about working smarter rather than harder. If you are involved in things you enjoy, your educational load won't seem like such a burden. Be sure to take time for self-care, such as sleep, unscheduled down time, and other activities that you find fun and energizing. See chapter 4 for more ways to relieve and avoid stress.

> "It has always seemed strange to me that in our endless discussions about education so little stress is laid on the pleasure of becoming an educated person, the enormous interest it adds to life. To be able to be caught up into the world of thought—that is, to be educated." —Edith Hamilton[14]

Summary

This chapter dove right in and talked about all the aspects of college and post-secondary schooling that you'll want to consider as you move forward. Remember that finding the right fit is especially important, as it increases the chances that you'll stay in school and finish your degree or program, as well as have an amazing experience while you're there. The careers covered in this book have varying educational requirements, which means that finding the right school can be very different depending on your career aspirations.

In this chapter, you learned about how to find a good educational fit and how to get the best education for the best deal. You also learned a little about scholarships and financial aid, how the SAT and ACT tests work, and how to write a unique personal statement that eloquently expresses your passions.

Use this chapter as a jumping off point to dig deeper into your particular area of interest. Some tidbits of wisdom to leave you with:

- If you need to, take the SAT and ACT tests early in your junior year so you have time to take them again. Most schools automatically accept the highest scores. Consider whether it would benefit you to leave off your SAT or ACT scores on your application, considering many universities' new "test-optional" policies.
- Make sure that the school you plan to attend has an accredited program in your field of study. This is particularly important in the health care field. Some professions follow national accreditation policies, while others are state-mandated and, therefore, differ across state lines. Do your research and understand the differences.
- Be sure to consider any hospital-sponsored degree programs in your area. There are many benefits to these programs—including a clearer path to employment. As with any program, just be sure they are accredited and that the hospital is well respected.
- Don't underestimate how important school visits are, especially in the pursuit of finding the right academic fit. Come prepared to ask questions not addressed on the school website or in the literature.
- Your personal statement is a very important piece of your application that can set you apart from others. Take the time and energy needed to make it unique and compelling.

- Don't assume you can't afford a school based on the "sticker price." Many schools offer great scholarships and aid to qualified students. It doesn't hurt to apply. This advice especially applies to minorities, veterans, and students with disabilities.
- Don't lose sight of the fact that it's important to pursue a career that you enjoy, are good at, and are passionate about! You'll be a happier person if you do so.

At this point, your career goals and aspirations should be gelling. At the least, you should have a plan for finding out more information. And don't forget about networking, which was covered in more detail in chapter 2. Remember to do the research about the school or degree program before you reach out and especially before you visit. Faculty and staff find students who ask challenging questions much more impressive than those who ask questions that can be answered by spending 10 minutes on the school website.

In chapter 4, we go into detail about the next steps—writing a résumé and cover letter, interviewing well, follow-up communications, and more. This is information you can use to secure internships, volunteer positions, summer jobs, and more. It's not just for college grads. In fact, the sooner you can hone these communication skills, the better off you'll be in the professional world.

4

Writing Your Résumé and Interviewing

*N*o matter which path you decide to take—whether you enter the workforce immediately after high school, go to college first and then find yourself looking for a job, or maybe do something in between, having a well-written résumé and impeccable interviewing skills will help you reach your ultimate goals. This chapter provides some helpful tips and advice to build the best résumé and cover letter, how to interview well with all your prospective employers, and how to communicate effectively and professionally at all times. All the advice in this chapter isn't just for people entering the workforce full time, either. It can help you score that internship or summer job or help you give a great college interview to impress the admissions office.

After we talk about writing your résumé, the chapter discusses important interviewing skills that you can build and develop over time. The chapter also has some tips for dealing successfully with stress, which is an inevitable byproduct of a busy life. Let's dive in!

Putting It All Together and Getting the Job

You've done your planning, your research, and you've chosen a career as a medical technician. You've prepared yourself with your education and training, and developed your practical skills as well as your knowledge of the job. And you know that being a medical technician is a great career with lots of opportunity. What are the next steps?

> "Far and away the best prize that life offers is the chance to work hard at work worth doing." —Theodore Roosevelt[1]

Finding and Applying for the Job

Of course, to apply for a job, you first have to know where to look for one. One of the quickest ways to find out what jobs are available in your field is to simply Google it (or search the internet with whichever search engine you like best)!

ONLINE JOB SITES

When companies want to hire new employees, they post job descriptions on job hunting or employee recruitment websites. These are a fantastic resource for you long before you're ready to actually apply for a job. You can read real job descriptions for real jobs and see what qualifications and experience are needed for the kinds of jobs that you're interested in. You'll also get a good idea of the range of salaries and benefits that go with different types of medical technician professions.

Pay attention to the required qualifications, of course, but also pay attention to the desired qualifications—these are the ones you don't have to have, but if you have them, you'll have an edge over other potential applicants.

Here are a few to get you started:

- www.monster.com
- www.indeed.com
- www.ziprecruiter.com
- www.glassdoor.com
- www.simplyhired.com

PROFESSIONAL ORGANIZATIONS

One of the services provided by most professional organizations is a list of open positions. Employers post jobs here because organization members are often the most qualified and experienced. The resources section in this book lists professional organizations for the different medical technician professions we've covered. You can also check online and talk to people in your field (such as your professors) to find out which organizations to join and where the best source of job information is likely to be.

NETWORKING

Some say the absolute best way to find a job is through networking. Your personal and professional contacts may know about an upcoming job that hasn't even been advertised yet. Sometimes, an employer may even create a position for someone they want to hire. Keep in touch with the people you know in the field, at every level, and let them know that you're available.

Still wondering about how to network? Flip back to chapter 2 and check out the section called "Networking" for some useful tips.

DANIELLE FULLER

Danielle Fuller.
Courtesy of Danielle Fuller.

About 15 years ago, Danielle Fuller was right out of college, working with horses. She was a barn manager. She had ridden horses for the Calgary and was in ROTC during college. Her original degree was a bachelor's of history/sociology and she wasn't sure what she wanted to do until she realized she could do medicine with horses! She worked with horses as a vet assistant for two years while pursuing her vet technology degree.

Because her husband traveled a lot, she moved from large animal to small animal practices while she was in veterinary technology school and continued to work in the Washington DC area as an assistant vet tech in a clinic setting. She got her degree in 2010 and then moved to Indiana. She started working at a local private veterinary office, where she still works part time. In July of 2019, she also took a job at VCA Advanced Veterinary Care Center, where she is an anesthesiologist for MRI and CT.

Can you talk about your current position?

In the standard clinic setting, I really enjoy assisting with surgeries. I especially enjoy dentistry, so I was able to do pretty much all the dental cleanings. I also assisted in lots of different surgeries, such as mass removals, spays, neuters, emergency surgeries.

We don't wellness at VCA, which is more like an animal hospital. I work mainly as the anesthesiologist for MRI, CT, and ultrasound. My job is called a *versa-tech* because I can jump into different departments, as needed. I can rotate through the ICW (intensive care ward), oncology department, and so on. I place IV catheters, help with fluids, patient care, and so on.

This is different medicine than I have been doing, because now I'm dealing with older and sicker patients. I like seeing so many aspects of vet medicine and am now learning new things. It's a lot of learning, which I enjoy!

Do you think education prepared you for your job?

Yes, I do. They have a couple of different options—online program or veterinary/ school setting. I did a little bit of both. There is lots of continuing education too. There are conferences and such, as well as online.

Most schools require you to work at or volunteer at a clinic before you get your degree, which is very helpful. I felt prepared because of this, with perhaps the exception of exotic animals. I did not get a lot of exotic and zoo medicine. You get a rotation of this, but it's not enough—but they do have a specialty in it. I've also been considering getting a specialty in vet technology for anesthesiology.

What's the best part of being a vet tech?

Taking care of animals. Making a difference in the pet's life and a family's life. With wellness especially, you are helping them have a healthy family member.

It's also a good, flexible profession for people with families. You can work different shifts and different positions, depending on the hours you need, and that can change over your career as your needs change too.

What are some issues in this profession that are especially challenging?

The biggest challenges for me are client expectations. Some get upset if the outcome isn't what they hoped for. Some animals come in very sick, and there are lots of emotions that happen. Euthanasia is difficult too.

What are some characteristics of a good vet tech?

People skills are important. You must be calm and handle pressure well. Steady hands are important, too! Multitasking is important. Vet techs help with physical therapy, dentistry, radiography, anesthesia, nursing care, and so on, which you wouldn't do really on the human side all at once. You have to learn all that. You're only as good as your weakest link.

What advice do you have for young people considering this career?

You should know that there are lots of aspects to veterinary medicine. Try to see as much of it as possible before you pick which path to go into. There is so much out there and many different paths, so look into the one that interests you the most.

How can a young person prepare for a career as a vet tech while in high school?

Many clinics allow kids to come in and job shadow. You can come in, tour, and see how it works. Volunteer where you can, such as at a shelter. They have age restrictions, but it usually is an option for high schoolers. Volunteer at a clinic, too; help clean up and see how it works there. Make sure you ask questions.

Any last thoughts?

Knowing how many possibilities there are in the veterinary medicine field is really helpful. Be sure to continue to learn—don't settle!

Writing Your Résumé

If you're a teen writing a résumé for your first job, you likely don't have a lot of work experience under your belt yet. Because of this limited work experience, you need to include classes and coursework that are related to the job you are seeking, as well as any school activities and volunteer experience you have. While you are writing your résumé, you might discover some talents and recall some activities you did that you forgot about, which are still important to add. Think about volunteer work, side jobs you've held (babysitting, dog walking, etc.), and the like.

The preferred type of résumé is usually a combination of the skills résumé and the reverse chronological résumé. The reverse chronological résumé is the most traditional format; it's written with the most current information first, going backwards to the oldest information last. The skills résumé (sometimes called a "functional résumé") is designed to highlight your skills and qualifications rather than your work history.

The combined résumé is the best of both worlds. It lets you highlight your most important skills and abilities, while also showing your employment history in order, from most recent to earliest job. The usual layout for a combined résumé is pretty simple.

- Name and contact information at the top
- Summary of your skills and abilities
- Education, starting with the most recently completed (if you have a college degree, it isn't necessary to include your high school). Note, once you've been employed for several years, you can move the education section to follow the experience section.
- Professional experience with job title, dates of employment (month or year is fine)
- Qualifications such as certification and licensing
- Awards and honors (if any)
- Volunteer experience (if relevant)

The first three entries above are pretty much standard, but the other entries can be creatively combined or developed to maximize your abilities and experience. These are not set-in-stone sections that every résumé must have.

If you're still not seeing the big picture here, it's helpful to look at student and part-time résumé examples online to see how others have approached this process. Search for "résumé examples" to get a look at some examples.

RÉSUMÉ-WRITING TIPS

Regardless of your situation and why you're writing the résumé, there are some basic tips and techniques you should use:

- Keep it short and simple. This includes using a simple, standard font and format. Using one of the résumé templates provided by your word processor software can be a great way to start.
- Use simple language. Keep it to one page.
- Highlight your academic achievements, such as a high GPA (above 3.5) or academic awards. If you have taken classes related to the job you're interviewing for, list those briefly as well.
- Emphasize your extracurricular activities, internships, and so on. These could include clubs, sports, dog walking, babysitting, or volunteer work. Use these activities to show your skills and abilities.

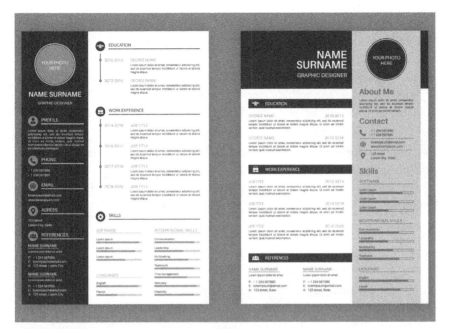

Your résumé documents your education and experience.
Olga Kurbatova/iStock/Getty Images

- Use action verbs, such as *led, created, taught, ran,* or *developed.*
- Be specific and give examples.
- Always be honest.
- Include leadership roles and experience.
- Edit and proofread at least twice and have someone else do the same. Ask a professional (such as your school writing center or your local library services) to proofread it for you also. Don't forget to run spell check.
- Include a cover letter (discussed next).

THE COVER LETTER

Every résumé you send out should include a cover letter. This can be the most important part of your job search because it's often the first thing that potential employers read. By including the cover letter, you're showing the employers that you took the time to learn about their organization and address them personally. This goes a long way to show that you're interested in the position.

A cover letter is also an opportunity to tell your story. It's a short, personalized letter that you send with your résumé to introduce yourself to a potential employer. A well-written cover letter is a way to show a little of your personality, to highlight where and how your background makes a good fit for the position you want, and to indicate your interest in working for that employer.

This letter should be brief. Introduce yourself and begin with a statement that will grab the person's attention. Keep in mind that they will potentially be receiving hundreds of résumés and cover letters for an open position. You want yours to stand out.

Your letter should be in business letter format (see the sidebar on "What Does a Business Letter Look Like?"). Important information to include in the cover letter, from the top, includes the following:

- The current date
- Your address and contact information
- The person's name, company, and contact information

Then you begin the letter portion of the cover letter, which should mention how you heard about the position, something extra about you that will interest the potential employer, practical skills you can bring to the position, and past experience related to the job. You should apply the facts outlined in your résumé to the job to which you're applying.

Each cover letter should be personalized for the position/company to which you're applying. Don't use "to whom it may concern." Instead, take the time to find out to whom you should actually address the letter. You should always try to send your letter and résumé together to the person who is responsible for making the hiring decision. If (and *only* if) you absolutely cannot find out who the decision maker is, then send them to the human resources office.

If you are emailing your cover letter instead of printing it out, you'll need to pay particular attention to the subject line of your email. Be sure that it is specific to the position you are applying for. In all cases, it's really important to follow the employer's instructions on how to submit your cover letter and résumé. Generally speaking, sending PDF documents rather than editable document forms is a better idea. For one, everyone can read a PDF, whereas they might not be able to read the version of the word-processing program that you used. Most word processing programs have an option under the save command that allows you to save your work as a PDF.

WHAT DOES A BUSINESS LETTER LOOK LIKE?

You'll be using a business-letter format for your cover letter and for your thank-you note. There are several options for what a business letter can look like. This one is considered the most business-like, so it's always a good choice. Always try to keep a business letter to a single page if you can.

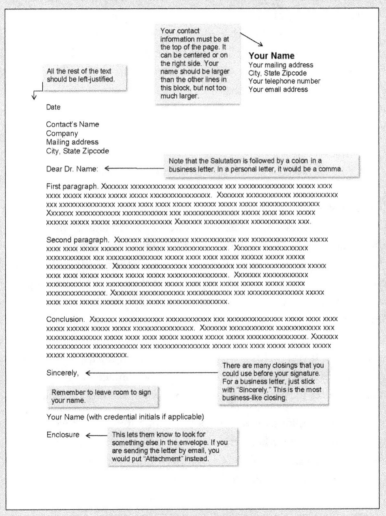

Sample cover letter

A few other tips about cover letters:

- Highlight your most relevant qualifications, such as skills that match the ones in the job description and/or skills that could transfer to those in the job description. Focus on your strengths and on what you could bring to the position. Think about this from the employer's point of view—what about your background will benefit them?
- Avoid negative language. Phrase everything in a positive way. In particular, avoid complaining about a previous employer.
- Your conclusion should include a confident call to action, such as requesting an interview. Don't ask directly for the job, just an interview at this point. Include your phone number here, as well as with your contact information at the top.
- Always sign the letter by hand.

Recommendations and References

In chapter 3, you learned about asking for letters of recommendation when you apply to college. Likewise, you'll need professional references when you apply for a job. Each employer may handle this request a little differently. Some will ask you to include contact information for your references (usually three separate individuals) when you apply, especially if they use an online application submission process. Others will expect you to supply that contact information at some later point—usually at or after your interview.

As far as what goes on your résumé, it's best to say that references are available on request. If you do list actual contacts, list no more than three and make sure you inform your contacts that they might be contacted.

Good choices for professional references would include the following:

- Previous employers who can speak to your abilities and work ethic
- Professors in your field, especially those who know you best
- Other professionals in the field, if they know you well and can speak to your qualifications and abilities

Personal contacts can make the difference! Don't be afraid to contact people you know. Personal connections can be a great way to find jobs and internship opportunities. Your high school teachers, your coaches and mentors, and your friends' parents are all examples of people who very well may know about jobs or internships that would suit you. Start asking several months before you hope to start a job or an internship, because it will take some time to do research and arrange interviews. You can also use social media in your search. LinkedIn, for example, includes lots of searchable information on local companies. Follow and interact with people on social media to get their attention. Just remember to act professionally and communicate with proper grammar, just as you would in person.

Interviewing Skills

The best way to avoid nerves and keep calm when you are interviewing is to be prepared. It's okay to feel scared, but keep it in perspective. It's likely that you'll receive many more rejections in your professional life than acceptances, as we all do. However, you only need one "yes" to start out. Think of the interviewing process as a learning experience. With the right attitude, you will learn from each experience and get better each subsequent interview. That should be your overarching goal. Consider these tips and tricks when interviewing, whether it be for a job, internship, college admission, or something else entirely:[2]

- Practice interviewing with a friend or relative. Practicing will help calm your nerves and make you feel more prepared. Ask for specific feedback from your friends. Do you need to speak louder? Are you making enough eye contact? Are you actively listening when the other person is speaking?
- Learn as much as you can about the company, school, or organization. Also be sure to understand the position for which you're applying. This will show the interviewer that you are motivated and interested in their organization.
- Speak up during the interview. Convey to the interviewer important points about you. Don't be afraid to ask questions. Try to remember the interviewers' names and call them by that.
- Arrive early and dress professionally and appropriately (you can read more about proper dress in a following section).

- Have good posture. Sit up straight, make reasonable eye contact, keep your shoulders back. Make it look normal, though—like you always sit or stand that way. Good posture conveys energy and enthusiasm for the job.
- Shake hands well. A firm handshake marks you as a person to be taken seriously. It's traditional to shake hands as you enter the meeting and again before you leave. (See the box on "To Shake or Not to Shake.")
- Take some time to prepare answers to commonly asked questions. Be ready to describe your career or educational goals to the interviewer.
- Be ready to ask questions. Some people don't like to ask questions in an interview because they think it makes them look ignorant. Actually, *not* asking questions makes them look uninterested. Have some questions prepared—both basic and more in depth, because the basic ones might get answered before you have a chance to ask them.
- Pay attention. If you're looking at your phone or out the window during an interview, you'll look like you don't care. Nobody wants to hire someone who doesn't care before the job even starts! Making (at least) intermittent eye contact helps show that you're paying attention.

Common questions you may be asked during a job interview include these:

- Tell me about yourself.
- What are your greatest strengths?
- What are your weaknesses?
- Tell me something about yourself that's not on your résumé.
- What are your career goals?
- How do you handle failure? Are you willing to fail?
- How do you handle stress and pressure?
- What are you passionate about?
- Why do you want to work for us?

Common questions you may be asked during a college admissions interview include these:

- Tell me about yourself.
- Why are you interested in going to college?
- Why do you want to major in this subject?
- What are your academic strengths?

- What are your academic weaknesses? How have you addressed them?
- What will you contribute to this college/school/university?
- Where do you see yourself in 10 years?
- How do you handle failure? Are you willing to fail?
- How do you handle stress and pressure?
- Whom do you most admire?
- What is your favorite book?
- What do you do for fun?
- Why are you interested in this college/school/university?

Jot down notes about your answers to these questions, but don't try to memorize the answers. You don't want to come off too rehearsed during the interview. Remember to be as specific and detailed as possible when answering these questions. Your goal is to set yourself apart in some way from the other people they will interview. Always accentuate the positive, even when you're asked about something you did not like, or about failure or stress. Most importantly, though, be yourself.

Active listening is the process of fully concentrating on what is being said, understanding it, and providing nonverbal cues and responses to the person talking.[3] It's the opposite of being distracted and thinking about something else when someone is talking. Active listening takes practice. You might find that your mind wanders and you need to bring it back to the person talking (and this could happen multiple times during one conversation). Practice this technique in regular conversations with friends and relatives. In addition to giving a better interview, it can cut down on nerves and make you more popular with friends and family, as everyone wants to feel that they are really being heard. (For more on active listening, check out https://www.mindtools.com/CommSkll/ActiveListening.htm.)

As mentioned, you should be ready to ask questions of your interviewer. In a practical sense, there should be some questions that you have that you can't find the answer to on the website or in the literature. Also, asking questions shows that you are interested and have done your homework. Avoid asking questions about salary/scholarships or special benefits at this stage, and don't

TO SHAKE OR NOT TO SHAKE?

A handshake is a traditional form of greeting, especially in business. When you arrive for a job interview—or just meet someone new—a good firm handshake shows that you are a person to be taken seriously.

But shaking hands is not done in every culture, and even in North America, the norm of shaking hands has changed. During the COVID-19 crisis that began in 2020, people stopped shaking hands in order to avoid spreading germs. As things get back to a new normal, some people will want to resume shaking hands and some people won't. There isn't one right answer here.

When you arrive for a job interview, follow the lead of the person you're meeting. A respectful head nod is just fine.

Shaking hands in the 21st century is something to think twice about.
Delmaine Donson/E +/Getty Images

ask about anything negative that you've heard about the company or school. Keep the questions positive and relative to you and the position to which you're applying. Some example questions to potential employers include these:

- What is a typical career path for a person in this position?
- How would you describe the ideal candidate for this position?
- How is the department organized?
- What kind of responsibilities come with this job? (Don't ask this if they've already addressed this question in the job description or discussion.)

- What can I do as a follow-up?
- When do you expect to reach a decision?

See the sidebar in chapter 3 entitled "Make the Most of School Visits" for some good example questions to ask the college admissions office. The important thing is to write your own questions related to answers you really want to know. This will show genuine interest. Be sure your question isn't answered on the website, in the job description, or in the literature.

Dressing Appropriately

It's important to determine what is actually appropriate in the setting of the interview. What is appropriate in a corporate setting might be different from what you'd expect as a small liberal arts college or at a large hospital setting. Most college admissions offices suggest "business casual" dress, for example, but depending on the job interview, you may want to step it up from there.

Even something like "business casual" can be interpreted in many ways, so do some research to find out what exactly is expected of you.
bernardbodo/iStock/Getty Images

Again, it's important to do your homework and come prepared. In addition to reading up on their guidelines, it never hurts to take a look around the site to see what other people are wearing to work or to interviews. Regardless of the setting, make sure your clothes are not wrinkled, untidy, or stained. Avoid flashy clothing of any kind.

Follow-Up Communication

Be sure to follow up, whether in email or via regular mail, with a thank-you note to the interviewer. This is true whether you're interviewing for a job or internship or interviewing with a college. A hand-written thank-you note, posted in the actual mail, is best. In addition to being considerate, it will trigger the interviewer's memory about you and it shows that you have genuine interest in the position, company, or school. Be sure to follow the business-letter format and highlight the key points of your interview and experience at the company/university. Make sure to be prompt with your thank-you! Put it in the mail the day after your interview (or send that email the same day).

What Employers Expect

Regardless of the job, profession, or field you end up working in, there are universal characteristics that all employers (and schools, for that matter) look for in potential employees. At this early stage in your professional life, you have an opportunity to recognize which of these foundational characteristics are your strengths (and therefore highlight them in an interview) and which are weaknesses (and therefore continue to work on them and build them up). Consider these universal characteristics that all employers look for:

- Positive attitude
- Dependability
- Desire to continue to learn
- Initiative
- Effective communication
- Cooperation
- Organization

This is not an exhaustive list, and other characteristics can very well include things like being sensitive to others, being honest, having good judgment, being loyal, being responsible, and being on time. Specifically, in health care, you can add having empathy, being detail-oriented, being flexible, having a caring nature, and being organized to that list. Consider these important characteristics when you answer the common questions that employers ask. It pays to work these traits into the answers, of course being honest and realistic about your abilities.

> *Beware the social media trap!* Prospective employers and colleges will check your social media sites, so make sure there is nothing too personal, explicit, or inappropriate on your sites. When you communicate out to the world in this way, don't use profanity and be sure to use proper grammar. Think about the version of yourself you are portraying online. Is it favorable or at least neutral to potential employers? They will look, rest assured.

Following Up

After any job interview, it is *extremely important* to follow up. This is what shows the company or institution that you are genuinely interested in the job. Write your thank-you note immediately after the interview. Be sure to mention your interest in the job and one or two things from the interview that were important in your conversation. If you met separately with several people, *send each one of them a separate note!*

While an email is less personal than a hand-signed letter on paper, it's a lot faster and today, it's considered an acceptable way to communicate. An email should have all the same content as a handwritten letter including (and especially) communicating your enthusiasm for the job.

Just like a handwritten note, start with "Dear Dr. Name" (replacing "Name" with whatever their name is, of course) and signing it "Sincerely," two line breaks, "Your Name." Since you won't be writing your signature, two line breaks are enough.

GETTING TO YES

Medical technicians are in demand, and you will most likely find a job, but there's no guarantee that you will be offered *the job you want most* when you first start looking. Here are some tips that will improve your chances of "getting to yes."

- Do your research. Find out about the company or institution that you want to apply to.
- Talk to people, especially people you know already or friends of friends who know something about that employer. Ask them these questions:

  ○ What is it like working for the potential employer?
  ○ What do they value in their employees?
  ○ What are the benefits?
  ○ What are the general pros and cons of working there?

- If there is a specific job opening that you're qualified for, apply for it!
- If there isn't a specific job opening, send a letter to the head of the company or department you're interested in, mention your contacts, and ask if they would have a conversation with you about potential openings.
- Be flexible. You might find a good job in a different location than you wanted or doing something slightly different than you originally planned.
- Put your best self forward. Everyone you meet is a potential contact for a job (or maybe just a new friend).
- Don't put all your eggs in one basket. Apply for many different jobs at the same time.

DEALING WITH NO

A wise person once said, "If they didn't hire you, you probably would not have been happy working there anyway." Both employers and employees need to find the right fit. If they didn't think you were the right fit, you most likely wouldn't have thought so after a while, either. Here are some tips to get you through a "no" while you're waiting for the "yes."

- Apply for lots of jobs at the same time, so no particular job will be too important to you.
- It doesn't feel great to be turned down for a job, but try not to take it personally.

- Don't burn your bridges! Don't retaliate with an angry letter or email, or troll the company all over social media. Another opportunity may come up there or with someone they know.
- Keep improving your résumé and your cover letter.
- Keep putting your best self forward. Even if you're feeling discouraged, pick up your head and go through your day shining with confidence.
- Work your contacts. Talk to other people you know. They may know an employer who would be a great match for you.
- Take advice. If someone (especially at or following an interview) tells you that you need to improve something, *improve it*. This may be an additional credential; it may be something about your interpersonal skills, your spelling, your breath, or whatever. If someone tells you something about yourself that you don't like to hear but suspect may be right, don't get mad. Get better.
- Keep doing your research, so if one employer turns you down, you have three more to apply to that day.
- Keep telling yourself that employment is just around the corner. Then make it true!

ON THE JOB

Now that you've got the job, it's important to keep it! It's not that hard. Just remember these simple tips:

- *Safety first*—Medical professionals deal with hazards all day long. Stay safe and watch out for the safety of those around you.
- *Do your best*—Your biggest asset is high-quality work.
- *Be reliable*—Your coworkers, clients, and supervisors will respect and appreciate you most when they know they can rely on you.
- *Be on time*—Show up on time for work or even a few minutes early.
- *Be prepared*—Walk in the door ready to work.
- *Keep good records*—This is important for safety as well as efficiency.
- *Be polite*—Treat everyone you meet with the same respect you want to receive.
- *Stay calm*—You do your best work when you're calm, especially if there's a problem to solve or an emergency.
- *Have integrity*—Be honest and respect other people's personal space and property.

EFFECTIVELY HANDLING STRESS

As you're forging ahead with your life plans, whether it's college, a full-time job, or even a gap year, you might find that these decisions feel very important and heavy and that the stress is difficult to deal with. First off, that's completely normal. Try these simple stress-relieving techniques:

- Take deep breaths in and out. Try this for 30 seconds. You'll be amazed at how it can help.
- Close your eyes and clear your mind.
- Go scream at the passing subway car or lock yourself in a closet and scream. Or scream into a pillow. For some people, this can really help.
- Keep the issue in perspective. Any decision you make now can be changed if it doesn't work out.

Want ways to avoid stress altogether? They are surprisingly simple. Of course, simple doesn't always mean easy, but it means they are basic and make sense with what we know about the human body:

- Get enough sleep
- Eat healthy
- Get exercise
- Go outside
- Schedule downtime
- Connect with friends and family

The bottom line is that you need to take time for self-care. There will always be conflict, but how you deal with it makes all the difference. This only becomes increasingly important as you enter college or the workforce and maybe have a family. Developing good, consistent habits related to self-care now will serve you all your life.

Summary

Well, you made it to the end of this book! Hopefully, you have learned enough about the medical technician field to start along your journey, or to continue with your path. If you've reached the end and you feel like being a med tech is right for you, that's great news. Or, if you've figured out that this isn't the right field for you, that's good information to learn too. For many of us, figuring out what we *don't* want to do and what we don't like are important steps in finding the right career.

There is a lot of good news about the medical tech field in this book! It's a very smart career choice for anyone with a passion to help people. It's fulfilling, lucrative, flexible, not monotonous, and easily customizable. Job demand is high and will continue to grow in the foreseeable future.

Whether you decide to attend a four-year university, get an associate degree, earn a certificate, or take a gap year, having a plan and an idea about your future can help guide your decisions. We hope that by reading this book, you are well on your way to having a plan for your future. Good luck to you as you move ahead!

With a little hard work and perseverance, you'll be on your way to career success!
djiledesign/iStock/Getty Images

Notes

Introduction

1. Bureau of Labor Statistics Occupational Outlook Handbook, "Diagnostic Medical Sonographers and Cardiovascular Technologists and Technicians, Including Vascular Technologists," https://www.bls.gov/ooh/healthcare/diagnostic-medical-sonographers.htm.

2. Bureau of Labor Statistics Occupational Outlook Handbook, "Nuclear Medicine Technologists," https://www.bls.gov/ooh/healthcare/nuclear-medicine-technologists.htm.

3. Bureau of Labor Statistics Occupational Outlook Handbook, "Phlebotomists," https://www.bls.gov/ooh/healthcare/phlebotomists.htm.

4. Bureau of Labor Statistics Occupational Outlook Handbook, "Clinical Laboratory Technologists and Technicians," https://www.bls.gov/ooh/healthcare/clinical-laboratory-technologists-and-technicians.htm.

5. Bureau of Labor Statistics Occupational Outlook Handbook, "Surgical Technologists," https://www.bls.gov/ooh/healthcare/surgical-technologists.htm.

6. Bureau of Labor Statistics Occupational Outlook Handbook, "Radiologic and MRI Technologists," https://www.bls.gov/ooh/healthcare/radiologic-technologists.htm.

7. https://www.bls.gov/ooh/healthcare/diagnostic-medical-sonographers.htm#tab-6

Chapter 1

1. "Cardiovascular Technologist/Technician," ExploreHealthCareers.org. https://explorehealthcareers.org/career/allied-health-professions/cardiovascular-technologist-technician/. Accessed July 14, 2021.

2. Ibid.

3. Bureau of Labor Statistics Occupational Outlook Handbook, "How to Become a Diagnostic Cardiovascular Technologist," https://www.bls.gov/ooh/healthcare/diagnostic-medical-sonographers.htm#tab-4. Accessed July 15, 2021.

4. CareerPlanner.org, "Cardiovascular Technologist Job Description," https://job-descriptions.careerplanner.com/Cardiovascular-Technologists-and-Technicians.cfm. Accessed July 15, 2021.

5. Bureau of Labor Statistics Occupational Outlook Handbook, "Diagnostic Medical Sonographers and Cardiovascular Technologists and Technicians, Including Vascular Technologists," https://www.bls.gov/ooh/healthcare/diagnostic-medical-sonographers.htm. Accessed July 15, 2021.

6. Ibid.

7. Bureau of Labor Statistics Occupational Outlook Handbook, "Nuclear Medicine Technologists," https://www.bls.gov/ooh/healthcare/nuclear-medicine-technologists.htm. Accessed July 15, 2021.

8. Ibid.

9. Ibid.

10. Bureau of Labor Statistics Occupational Outlook Handbook, "How to Become a Phlebotomist," https://www.bls.gov/ooh/healthcare/phlebotomists.htm#tab-4. Accessed July 16, 2021.

11. Ibid.

12. Bureau of Labor Statistics Occupational Outlook Handbook, "Phlebotomists," https://www.bls.gov/ooh/healthcare/phlebotomists.htm#tab-1. Accessed July 16, 2021.

13. Bureau of Labor Statistics Occupational Outlook Handbook, "Clinical Laboratory Technologists and Technicians," https://www.bls.gov/ooh/healthcare/clinical-laboratory-technologists-and-technicians.htm. Accessed July 16, 2021.

14. Ibid.

15. Ibid.

16. Ibid.

17. Bureau of Labor Statistics Occupational Outlook Handbook, "What Surgical Technologists Do," https://www.bls.gov/ooh/healthcare/surgical-technologists.htm#tab-2. Accessed July 16, 2021.

18. Bureau of Labor Statistics Occupational Outlook Handbook, "How to Become a Surgical Technologist," https://www.bls.gov/ooh/healthcare/surgical-technologists.htm#tab-4. Accessed July 16, 2021.

19. Bureau of Labor Statistics Occupational Outlook Handbook, "What Surgical Technologists Do," https://www.bls.gov/ooh/healthcare/surgical-technologists.htm#tab-2. Accessed July 16, 2021.

20. Ibid.

21. Bureau of Labor Statistics Occupational Outlook Handbook, "What Radiologic and MRI Technologists Do," https://www.bls.gov/ooh/healthcare/radiologic-technologists.htm#tab-2. Accessed July 16, 2021.

22. Ibid.

23. Bureau of Labor Statistics Occupational Outlook Handbook, "Radiologic and MRI Technologists," https://www.bls.gov/ooh/healthcare/radiologic-technologists .htm#tab-1. Accessed July 16, 2021.

Chapter 2

1. "What Is the Process of Becoming an X-Ray Technician?" https://www .cambridgehealth.edu/blog/what-is-the-process-of-becoming-an-x-ray-technician/. Accessed July 21, 2021.

2. Bureau of Labor Statistics Occupational Outlook Handbook, "What Radio-logic and MRI Technologists Do," https://www.bls.gov/ooh/healthcare/radiologic -technologists.htm#tab-2. Accessed July 16, 2021.

3. "State Licensing," https://www.arrt.org/pages/about-the-profession/state -licensing. Accessed July 21, 2021.

4. "New Survey Reveals 85% of All Jobs Are Filled Via Networking," LinkedIn .com, https://www.linkedin.com/pulse/new-survey-reveals-85-all-jobs-filled-via-net working-lou-adler/.

5. "Leverage Your Volunteering Experience When Applying to School," New GradPhysicalTherapy.com, https://newgradphysicaltherapy.com/volunteer-experi ence-physical-therapy-school.

Chapter 3

1. Gap Year Association, "Gap Year Data and Benefits," https://www.gapyear association.org/data-benefits.php

2. *US News & World Report*, "Finding a Good College Fit," https://www .usnews.com/education/blogs/the-college-admissions-insider/2011/06/13/finding-a -good-college-fit.

3. National Center for Education Statistics, "Fast Facts: Graduation Rates," n.d., https://nces.ed.gov/fastfacts/display.asp?id=40.

4. US Department of Education, "Focusing Higher Education on Student Success," https://www.ed.gov/news/press-releases/fact-sheet-focusing-higher-educa tion-student-success.

5. Ibid.

6. FairTest, https://fairtest.org/university/optional. "1,425+ Accredited, 4-Year Colleges & Universities with ACT/SAT-Optional Testing Policies for Fall, 2022 Admis-sions." Last updated May 17, 2021. Accessed May 21, 2021.

7. Allison Wignall, "Preference of the ACT or SAT by State (Infographic)." CollegeRaptor. https://www.collegeraptor.com/getting-in/articles/act-sat/prefer ence-act-sat-state-infographic/ November 14, 2019.

8. https://blog.prepscholar.com/which-schools-use-the-common-application -complete-list.

9. BigFuture, "Focus on Net Price, Not Sticker Price." CollegeBoard. https:// bigfuture.collegeboard.org/pay-for-college/paying-your-share/focus-on-net-price-not -sticker-price.

10. Jennifer Ma, Sandy Baum, Matea Pender, and C. J. Libassi. *Trends in College Pricing 2019* (New York: College Board, 2019). https://research.collegeboard.org/pdf /trends-college-pricing-2019-full-report.pdf.

11. Ibid.

12. https://research.collegeboard.org/trends/college-pricing/figures-tables/aver age-net-price-sector-over-time.

13. Federal Student Aid, An Office of the US Department of Education, "FAFSA Changes for 2017–2018," https://studentaid.ed.gov/sa/about/announce ments/fafsa-changes.

14. Edith Hamilton, quoted in the *Saturday Evening Post*, September 27, 1958.

Chapter 4

1. Theodore Roosevelt, from a speech in New York, September 7, 1903; twenty-sixth president of United States (1858–1919).

2. Justin Ross Muchnick, *Teens' Guide to College & Career Planning*, 12th ed. (Lawrenceville, NJ: Peterson's Publishing, 2015), pp. 179–80.

3. Mind Tools, "Active Listening: Hear What People Are Really Saying," https:// www.mindtools.com/CommSkll/ActiveListening.htm.

Glossary

accreditation: The act of officially recognizing an organizational body, person, or educational facility as having a particular status or being qualified to perform a particular activity. For example, schools and colleges are accredited. (See also *certification.*)

ACT: The American College Test (ACT) is one of the standardized college entrance tests that anyone wanting to enter undergraduate studies in the United States should take. It measures knowledge and skills in mathematics, English, reading, and science reasoning, as they apply to college readiness. There are four multiple-choice sections. There is also an optional writing test. The total score of the ACT is 36. (See also *SAT.*)

active listening: The process of fully concentrating on what is being said, understanding it, and providing nonverbal cues and responses to the person talking. It's the opposite of being distracted and thinking about something else when someone is talking to you.

allied health professionals: Trained health professionals who are not doctors, dentists, or nurses. This is a large area and includes the professions covered in this book, as well as speech therapists, nutritionists, emergency medical technicians (EMTs) and paramedics, and medical assistants, to name a few. They provide services pertaining to the diagnosis, evaluation, and prevention of diseases and disorders.

anatomy: The area of science concerned with the bodily structure and organization of humans, animals, and other living things.

anesthesia: The giving of medicine so that surgery and other medical procedures can be performed on patients without them feeling any pain, and in many situations, without patients being awake or conscious during the procedure. There are many types of anesthesia.

associate degree: A degree awarded by community or junior colleges that typically requires two years of study.

baby boomers: The American generation that was born after World War II, starting in about 1945, until about 1964. During this time, there was a "boom" (large increase) in the number of births in the United States. This matters to professionals in health care, because baby boomers continue to age and disproportionally need care and services that they provide.

bachelor's degree: An undergraduate degree awarded by colleges and universities that is typically a four-year course of study when pursued full-time, but this can vary by degree earned and by the university awarding the degree.

cardiopulmonary resuscitation (CPR): Treatment given by a certified professional to a person who has collapsed, has no discernable pulse, and has stopped breathing. It involves giving the victim external cardiac massage and breaths into the lungs in order to restore oxygen intake and blood circulation.

cardiovascular system: The system of the human body making up the heart and blood, including veins and arteries. Applicable diseases include stroke, heart attack, and high blood pressure.

certification: The action or process of confirming certain skills or knowledge on a person. Usually provided by some third-party review, assessment, or educational body. Individuals, not organizations, are certified. (See also *accreditation*.)

computerized tomography (CT) scan: A computed tomography scan (often called a CT scan or a CAT scan) is a painless medical imaging technique that produces detailed images of the body (both soft tissue areas and bones) for diagnostic purposes. These are done noninvasively, which means they do not have to cut into a patient to get the images. The medical professionals who perform CT scans are often called radiographers, radiology technologists, or X-ray techs.

defibrillator: A device that checks the heart's rhythm and sends a shock to the heart to restore its normal rhythm. The device is used to help people having a sudden cardiac arrest (heart attack).

diagnosis: When a health care professional determines the nature of an illness or problem after examining a patient.

diagnostic lab: A laboratory where tests are carried out on specimens (such as blood, tissue, and other bodily fluids) to help in diagnosis, treatment, and prevention of disease.

doctorate degree: The highest level of degree awarded by colleges and universities. Qualifies the holder to teach at the university level. Requires (usually published) research in the field. Typically requires an additional three to five years of study after earning a bachelor's degree. Anyone with a doctorate degree can be addressed as a "doctor," not just medical doctors.

ECG (or EKG) technicians: Health care professionals who perform diagnostic tests in order to help doctors identify cardiovascular problems in patients. The tests can be used to help discover any irregularities in the heart that could lead to a heart attack or heart disease. ECG technicians work mostly in hospitals, but they can also work in long-term specialty care facilities or private practices. (See also *radiologic technicians*.)

electrocardiogram (ECG or EKG): A simple test that can be used to check the heart's rhythm and electrical activity. Sensors attached to the skin are used to detect the electrical signals produced by the heart each time it beats. A standard or "resting" ECG is one of the simplest and fastest tests used to evaluate the heart. See also *Holter monitor.*

EMT/EMS: Emergency medical technicians (EMTs) work in the emergency medical service (EMS) profession. They are specifically trained and certified to treat the sick and injured in emergency situations. They respond to emergency 911 calls by performing medical services as they are transporting patients to medical facilities.

gap year: A gap year is a year between high school and college (or sometimes between college and postgraduate studies) whereby the student is not in school but is instead typically involved in volunteer programs, such as the Peace Corps, AmeriCorps, in travel experiences, or in work and teaching experiences.

gerontology: The study of old age.

grants: Money to pay for postsecondary education that is typically awarded to students who have financial needs, but can also be used in the areas of athletics, academics, demographics, veteran support, and special talents. Grants do not have to be paid back.

Holter monitor: A type of portable electrocardiogram (ECG). It records the electrical activity of the heart continuously over 24 hours or longer while the patient is away from the doctor's office. (See also *electrocardiogram.*)

kinesiology: The study of how the body moves and the mechanics of its movement.

license: An official document, card, certificate, and so on, that gives you permission to have, use, or do something, such as practice as a dental hygienist. Typically, one gets certified and then applies for a license.

master's degree: A secondary degree awarded by colleges and universities that requires at least one additional year of study after obtaining a bachelor's degree. The degree holder shows mastery of a specific field.

medical technicians: A *technician* typically needs an associate degree in medical lab technology or a related field, or, perhaps, a nondegree certificate. Technicians usually serve in more entry-level positions and may report to a medical technologist.

medical technologists: A *technologist* usually needs a bachelor's degree and/or a more extensive knowledgebase than a technician. Technologists usually have more experience and more responsibility and earn greater pay than technologists.

MRI technologists: Health care professionals who work in radiology departments and manage the use of magnetic resonance imaging scanners (MRIs), which use radio waves as well as a magnetic field to create images of a patient's organs and tissues to diagnose injuries and disease. (See also *radiologic technicians.*)

oncology: The branch of medicine that deals with the study, prevention, diagnosis, and treatment of cancer and/or tumors.

operating room technicians: Health care professionals who assist surgeons during operations. They prepare operating rooms by setting up surgical instruments and equipment and preparing sterile solutions and medications. They are also called surgical technologists.

pacemaker: A small device that's placed under the skin in a patient's chest to help control their heartbeat. It's used to help the heart beat more regularly.

pathology: The science that identifies and manages diseases.

personal statement: A written description of your accomplishments, outlook, interest, goals, and personality that's an important part of your college application. The personal statement should set you apart from others. The required length depends on the institution, but they generally range from 1 to 2 pages, or 500 to 1,000 words.

phlebotomy technicians (or phlebotomists): Health care professionals who draw blood from patients for tests, transfusions, research, and blood donations.

physician assistant (PA): PAs are licensed to diagnose and treat illness and disease and to prescribe medication to patients. They work in physician offices, hospitals, and clinics in collaboration with a licensed physician. Their education, which is more in line with the medical model, requires a bachelor's of science, a 25-month accredited physician assistant program, and a one-year clinical rotation.

positron emission tomography (PET) scan: A PET scan is an imaging test that helps show how a patient's tissues and organs are functioning. Techs use a radioactive drug (a tracer) to show this activity. A PET scan can sometimes detect disease before it shows up on other imaging tests.

postsecondary degree: The educational degree above and beyond a high school education. This is a general description that includes trade certificates and certifications, associate degrees, bachelor's degrees, master's degrees, and beyond.

PTSD (posttraumatic stress disorder): An anxiety disorder that can be the result of experiencing a traumatic event. People suffering from PTSD may have intense fear, helplessness, guilt, and stress, long after an event is over. They often relive these events in their mind and suffer from flashbacks.

radiologic technicians: Health care professionals who perform diagnostic imaging procedures, such as X-ray examinations, magnetic resonance imaging (MRI) scans, and computed tomography (CT) scans.

radiopharmaceuticals: These are biological molecules that include radioactive isotopes in them. They can be used to target specific organs, tissues, or cells in the human body. These radioactive drugs can be used for the diagnosis and, increasingly, for the therapy of diseases such as cancer. Nuclear medicine technologists work with radioactive drugs to help physicians and surgeons diagnose a patient's condition. They usually inject radiopharmaceuticals into the bloodstream of a patient.

rehabilitation: The process of returning someone back to a healthier state, better health, or a more functional life after an illness or accident.

SAT: The Scholastic Aptitude Test (SAT) is one of the standardized tests in the United States that those applying to undergraduate studies should take. It measures verbal and mathematical reasoning abilities as they relate to predicting successful performance in college. It is intended to complement a student's GPA and school record in assessing readiness for college. The total score of the SAT is 1600. (See also *ACT*.)

scholarships: Merit-based aid used to pay for postsecondary education that does not have to be paid back. Scholarships are typically awarded based on academic excellence or some other special talent, such as music or art.

stent: A metal or plastic tube inserted into a vessel or duct (such as a narrowed artery) to keep the passageway open.

X-ray technicians: See radiologic technicians.

Further Resources

Are you looking for more information about the medical technologist field or even about a branch within health care in general? Do you want to know more about the college application process or need some help finding the right educational fit for you? Do you want a quick way to search for a good college or school? Try these resources as a starting point on your journey toward finding a great career!

Books

Field, Shelly. *Career Opportunities in Health Care,* 3rd ed. New York: Checkmark Books, 2007.

Fiske, Edward. *Fiske Guide to Colleges.* Naperville, IL: Sourcebooks, Inc., 2018.

Gresham, Barbara B. *Today's Health Professions: Working Together to Provide Quality Care.* Philadelphia: F.A. Davis Co., 2016.

Le Baudour, Chris and J. David Bergeron. *Emergency Medical Responder: First on Scene*, 10th ed. Hoboken, NJ: Pearson, 2015.

Muchnick, Justin Ross. *Teens' Guide to College & Career Planning*, 12th ed. Lawrenceville, NJ: Peterson's Publishing, 2015.

Princeton Review. *The Best 382 Colleges, 2018 Edition: Everything You Need to Make the Right College Choice.* New York: The Princeton Review, 2018.

Strock, James. *Serve to Lead 2.0: Twenty-first Century Leaders Manual,* 2nd ed. Scotts Valley, CA: CreateSpace Independent Publishing Platform, 2018.

Websites

Accrediting Bureau of Health Education Schools
www.abhes.org
This accrediting agency is recognized by the US Department of Education and by the Council for Higher Education Accreditation. The website includes

a list of accredited institutions and programs, a calendar of upcoming events, a special tab for students, a section on recent publications, and much more.

The American Association of Medical Assistants
www.aama-ntl.org
This organization certifies people to become Certified Medical Assistants (CMAs) through their national CMA exam. Their mission is to provide medical assistant professionals with education, certification, credential acknowledgment, networking opportunities, and advocacy.

American Gap Year Association
gapyearassociation.org
The American Gap Year Association's mission is "making transformative gap years an accessible option for all high school graduates." A gap year is a year taken between high school and college to travel, teach, work, volunteer, generally mature, and otherwise experience the world. Their website has lots of advice and resources for anyone considering taking a gap year.

American Medical Technologists (AMT)
https://americanmedtech.org
Offers various certifications for laboratory consultants, medical laboratory assistants, and molecular diagnostic technologists, as well as support and advocacy.

American Registry for Diagnostic Medical Sonographers (ARDMS)
www.ardms.org
This nonprofit organization administers exams and awards credentials in the areas of ultrasound. Through its mission, ARDMS empowers sonographers to provide exceptional patient care through rigorous assessments and continual learning.

The American Registry of Radiologic Technologists
www.arrt.org
The American Registry of Radiologic Technologists certifies people operating medical imaging equipment. It's the world's largest organization offering

credentials in medical imaging, interventional procedures, and radiation therapy. They certify and register technologists in a range of disciplines.

American Society for Clinical Laboratory Science
www.ascls.org
This organization works to advance the expertise of clinical laboratory professionals to deliver quality, consumer-focused, outcomes-oriented clinical laboratory services. Claims more than 9,000 clinical laboratory professional, student, and educator members in more than 50 state and regional areas.

The Balance Website
www.thebalance.com
This site is all about managing money and finances, but also has a large section called Your Career, which provides advice for writing résumés and cover letters, interviewing, and more. Search the site for teens and you can find teen-specific advice and tips.

Cardiovascular Credentialing International
www.cci-online.org
An independent not-for-profit organization created for the purpose of administering credentialing examinations as an independent credentialing agency, as well as to provide support and advocacy.

College Board Website
www.collegeboard.org
The College Entrance Examination Board tracks and summarizes financial data from colleges and universities all over the United States. This site can be your one-stop shop for all things college research. It contains lots of advice and information about taking and doing well on the SAT and ACT tests, many articles on college planning, a robust college searching feature, a scholarship searching feature, and a major and career search area. You can type your career of interest (for example, occupational therapy) into the search box and get back a full page that describes the career, gives advice on how to prepare, where to get experience, how to pay for it, what characteristics you should have to excel in this career, lists of helpful classes to take while in high school, and lots of links for more information. A great, well-organized site.

College Grad Career Profile Website
www.collegegrad.com/careers

Although this site is primarily geared toward college graduates, the careers profile area, indicated above, has a list of links to nearly every career you could ever think of. A single click takes you to a very detailed, helpful section that describes the job in detail, explains the educational requirements, includes links to good colleges that offer this career, includes links to actual open jobs and internships, describes the licensing requirements, if any, lists salaries, and much more.

Commission on Accreditation of Allied Health Education Programs
www.caahep.org

One of the largest programmatic accreditors in the health sciences field. The website enables you to easily search through a large collection of accredited programs. It also includes a specific section just for students and a news and events section.

Explore Health Careers Website
www.explorehealthcareers.org

As the title suggests, this site enables you to explore careers in the health fields. You can seek answers to questions such as whether a career in health is right for you or not, find the right fit and focus your search within the many fields, actually find the job or internship you're looking for, learn more about paying for college, and more.

Khan Academy
www.khanacademy.org

The Khan Academy website is an impressive collection of articles, courses, and videos about many educational topics in math, science, and the humanities. You can search any topic or subject (by subject matter and grade), and read lessons, take courses, and watch videos to learn all about it. Includes test prep information for the SAT, ACT, AP, GMAT, and other standardized tests. There is also a college admissions tab with lots of good articles and information, provided in the approachable Khan style.

Live Career Website
www.livecareer.com

This site has an impressive number of resources directed toward teens for writing résumés, cover letters, and interviewing.

Mapping Your Future
www.mappingyourfuture.org
This site helps young people figure out what they want to do and maps out how to reach career goals. Includes helpful tips on résumé writing, job hunting, job interviewing, and more.

Monster
www.monster.com
Perhaps the most well-known, and certainly one of the largest employment websites in the United States. You fill in a couple of search boxes and away you go! You can sort by job title, of course, as well as by company name, location, salary range, experience range, and much more. The site also includes information about career fairs, advice on résumés and interviewing, and more.

Occupational Outlook Handbook by the Bureau of Labor Statistics
www.bls.gov
The US Bureau of Labor Statistics produces this website. It offers lots of relevant and updated information about various careers, including average salaries, how to work in the industry, the job's outlook in the job market, typical work environments, and what workers do on the job. See www.bls.gov/emp/ for a full list of employment projections.

Peterson's College Prep Website
www.petersons.com
In addition to lots of information about preparing for the ACT and SAT tests and easily searchable information about scholarships nationwide, Peterson's site includes a comprehensive searching feature to search for universities and schools based on location, major, name, and more.

Study.Com Website
www.study.com
This site is similar to Khan Academy, where you can search any topic or subject and read lessons, take courses, and watch videos to learn all about it.

It includes a good collection of information about health care and the basic science and medicine needed to excel in postsecondary school courses.

TeenLife: College Preparation
www.teenlife.com

This organization calls itself "the leading source for college preparation," and it includes lots of information about summer programs, gap year programs, community service, and more. They believe that spending time out "in the world" outside of the classroom can help students develop important life skills. This site contains lots of links to volunteer and summer programs.

US News & World Report College Rankings
www.usnews.com/best-colleges

US News & World Report provides almost 50 different types of numerical rankings and lists of colleges throughout the United States to help students with their college search. You can search colleges by best reviewed, best value for the money, best liberal arts schools, best schools for B students, and more.

About the Author

Kezia Endsley is an editor and author from Indianapolis, Indiana. In addition to editing technical publications and writing books for teens, she enjoys running and triathlons, traveling, reading, and spending time with her family and many pets.

CPSIA information can be obtained
at www.ICGtesting.com
Printed in the USA
LVHW041644221222
735786LV00003B/495

9 781538 159286